"Given the large number of changes impacting our industry, it is essential to have a unifying document or vision for the work of volunteers. The strategy and framework which Rich has developed in *Connections* will serve as that unifying vision."

—Bill McKenna, CSP,
  Book Division Manager,
  Boston University Bookstore,
  660 Corporation, Boston, MA

"This is not just a 'bookstore thing.' *Connections* addresses many of the issues industry suppliers have discussed for years. It's absolutely required reading. It pulls everyone in the college market together, from publishers to vendors to store people to the campus community, all in one quick read."

—Dick Welsh, Director, College
  Market, Avery Dennison,
  Chicopee, MA

"Rich McDaniel is one of our industry's most cogent thinkers about the uncertain future we face. This book shows how to take steps now that will enable you to meet the coming challenges with more confidence. "

—Bob Follett, Counselor, Follett
  Corporation, River Grove, IL

"A well written book gives a manager a lot of information to think about - information on which to base decisions. As a manager of a small bookstore for over 15 years, I've seen we have a tendency to act on our decisions as if we were still back in the '70s. It is true some things don't change, however, a lot of things have changed and this book just lets us decide for ourselves how we will connect in the present and in the future. Well done..."

—Alex Aragon, CSP, Director,
  Eastern New Mexico University
  Bookstore, Portales, NM

"Rich has properly identified the key stakeholders with whom connections must be made and has as well put forth a simple and doable plan that can help the industry move toward achieving the strategy."

—John Marcus, CSP, Chairman/
  CEO, Matthews Medical/CBA
  Bookstores, St. Louis, MO

"*Connections: NACS and You* is clear, concise and makes perfect sense. I encourage everyone to read it. As technology is so rapidly changing our lives, it is even more important to forge new and stronger connections with our colleagues, our customers and our future."

—Judy Leavitt, Manager, Chemeketa Community College Bookstore, Salem, OR

"'Connections' activities are the cobblestones of the path to the future. If a store implements even a few of the suggestions from this plan, it will be far better positioned to deal with present challenges as well as future ones. Just do it! It's a great plan and the time is right."

—Pamela Mills, CSP, General Manager, University Bookstore, Iowa State University, Ames, IA

"*Connections* is visionary in scope, yet accessible and practical. The message is insightful and compelling, the presentation is succinct and enjoyable, and perhaps most important, the suggested actions are doable by anyone."

—William P. Simpson, President/ General Manager, UConn Co-op, University of Connecticut, Storrs, CT

"*Connections* is an outstanding and necessary strategy for individual stores. It also provides a strong framework from which NACS can develop our own strategy of serving member college stores. The Association, too, must 'connect' with our members, our employees, our suppliers, and our community as we carry out our philosophy of doing all that we can to help college stores succeed and compete in a rapidly changing world. I commend Rich McDaniel, Tommye Miller and the entire NACS Board for their leadership in bringing the *Connections* theme to the industry and for pledging multi-year support for the effort. I pledge the support of the NACS and NACSCORP staff in supporting these efforts and in working with them to create an association strategic plan based on the same theme. The bottom line is that stores adopting the strategy will be in a much stronger position for success than those that do not, and the exact same thing can be said about associations."

—Garis F. Distelhorst, CAE, Chief Staff Executive, NACS, Oberlin, OH

"*Connections: NACS and You* will insure that college store managers will know how to take time today to prepare for tomorrow, as we all work to connect with our Customers, Campus, Vendors, and Coworkers."

—Barbara Miller Heron, Manager, The Skidmore Shop, Skidmore College, Saratoga Springs, NY

"I hope *Connections* will wake up college store personnel. The material in this publication is not new to the industry, but many college stores have not reached out to their university's family. Unless the store gets involved with the academic, auxiliary, athletic, library and student organizations on their campus, they have closed their door to maintaining an institutional operation."

—Mary L. Bonach, CSP, Director, The Book Center, University of Pittsburgh, PA

"In today's world it comes down to this: if you don't connect with the customers, staff, faculty and vendors, your business will slowly but surely die. To have an association and not connect with your members is a pure waste of time and effort of a lot of people who want to succeed."

—Michael Bare, CSP, Manager, Coastline Community College Bookstore, Fountain Valley, CA

"I have discussed partnering and campus relationships with my staff for a number of years. The importance of the Connections strategy is that it expands the idea to include our co-workers and the vendors with whom we work. It shows ways NACS can support stores both large and small. I encourage all managers to read and share with staff."

—Elroy Littlefield, Director Bookstore Services, Hornet Bookstore, California State University, Sacramento, CA

"This easily read book identifies many critical issues facing us in our stores, in our businesses, on our campuses, and in the world, and it provides a host of surprisingly simple approaches to make us better managers for the future. *Connections* is about networking with vision, purpose, and focus, and on a very broad scale. We'll definitely be using it in our store as we prepare for and confront the future. I encourage you to read it!"

—Bob McCampbell, Director, Bay Tree Bookstore, University of California/Santa Cruz, Santa Cruz, CA

RICHARD W. MCDANIEL, CSP

CONNECTIONS:

NACS & YOU

Connections: NACS & You presents the vision of the NACS leadership and is the framework for developing tangible actionable initiatives at all levels throughout the industry. The book is published by NACS with the support of the College Stores Research and Educational Foundation through grants from Arrowhead Distributors and Xerox Corporation.

NACS Mission:

The mission of the National Association of College Stores is to be the unified voice for all college stores and to deliver educational opportunities, services, and products that college stores and their suppliers need to effectively serve higher education.

Connections: NACS and You
ISBN: 0-942855-55-8

Production Notes: This book was created in PageMaker 4.2 and Freehand 4.0. It was
printed on the Xerox DocuTech Network Publisher Model 135. The cover was created in
Freehand 4.0 and printed on the Xerox 5775 SSE Digital Color Copier/Printer.

For Information and Additional Copies:
National Association of College Stores, 500 East Lorain Street, Oberlin, OH 44074
PHONE: 216/775-7777; FAX: 216/775-4769; INTERNET: info@nacs.org

ACKNOWLEDGEMENTS

This work is built upon the insights of many of our industry's leaders, graciously contributed during the ongoing development of NACS' strategic initiatives. The list of participants, although too long to acknowledge individually, includes members of the NACS, NACSCORP and CSREF boards, their key staff, many state and regional association leaders, and representatives from several distinguished corporations.

It also represents careful collaboration with 1993-94 NACS President, Pam Mills, whose leadership has laid the foundation upon which I build, President-Elect Tommye Miller, whose commitment to follow through will dramatically impact the success of today's initiatives, and NACS' chief staff officer, Garis Distelhorst, whose commitment provides much-needed continuity as volunteer officers come and go.

Similarly, I am grateful to close colleagues Bill Simpson, Will Connor, and in a special way Gary Shapiro, whose penetrating analysis, constant innovation, and unwavering support have molded so many of my views. And special thanks go to all of the NACS and CSREF staff members who have dedicated much time and expertise in coordinating revisions, design, production and distribution of this document.

Most of all, I want to acknowledge my colleagues at the Cornell Campus Store, who have supported and often endured almost two decades of constant experimentation, and whose outstanding capabilities made it possible for me to accept the role of NACS President. We have savored together many sweet successes, many of which were preceded by a long struggle You are very special people!

Finally, to you, the NACS membership, I am particularly indebted, both for the privilege of leadership, and the even greater privilege of friendship.

THE DOCUMENT COMPANY
XEROX

Xerox Corporation is pleased to have helped deliver the message of *Connections: NACS and You* to members of the college store industry. This is a crucial time for industry members to prepare for the future, and connecting to key stakeholders by developing results-oriented relationships is the surest way to meet the challenges of the future.

The production of the book you hold in your hands has been an excellent example of the spirit of *Connections*. The contents were transported electronically among the people who assisted in editing and formatting, achieving savings in time, and expenses in shipping and paper. By communicating up front about the most effective way to produce the book, Xerox and NACS were able to select 5 $1/2$" x 8 $1/2$" as a final trim size, which maximizes the throughput of the DocuTech, and results in a convenient size for the reader. In addition, Xerox and NACS collaborated on the design of the color cover prior to its production on the 5775 Digital Color Copier Printer.

Xerox is an industry leader in digital printing and document services, including solutions developed specifically for the college store market. Our systems such as DocuTech Network Publisher, 5775, and Xerox Documents on Demand will enable you to respond effectively to the rapid movement toward custom publishing and demand printing of books and other instructional materials. *Connections* is an excellent example of this exciting new form of document production.

Xerox Corporation looks forward to working with our colleagues in the higher education industry to meet the challenges described in *Connections*, and has been pleased to assist the College Stores Research & Educational Foundation in producing this book.

Glenn Alexander, Manager, Education Industry Marketing
XEROX CORPORATION

Arrowhead Distributors is delighted to be assisting in the production and distribution of *Connections: NACS and You.* Rich's book describes a framework that we believe will be very helpful for NACS members to use in planning for the future.

In addition to providing the latest technology in computers, software and comsumer electronics for resale, Arrowhead is committed to providing education, support and communication to help our customers be successful. As a vendor which sells to both mass merchandisers and college stores, we are well aware of the challenges that all types of retailers face. Sell-through of our products depends very much on individual stores' marketing and merchandising efforts, so we need to work together to offer feedback and support in order to have lasting, mutually successful, relationships.

Arrowhead supports NACS and CSREF in their efforts to promote the Connections strategy and assist individual stores in creating "to do" lists for building win-win alliances. In our relationships with college stores, we strive for the type of cooperation that Rich calls for so clearly:

> "It is in the interest of both the store and the vendor/publisher to cooperate fully as partners in order to understand and sell to the ultimate customers: students, faculty, staff, alumni, and campus visitors. In fact, high stock turnover rates, attractive merchandising, good customer service, fair pricing, effective promotions, and all other typically 'retail' concerns are as crucial to suppliers as they are to stores." (p. 49)

We commend NACS' leadership for the hard work and many hours of effort that it has taken to develop the dynamic and refreshing view presented in *Connections,* and support the industry as it puts this view into practice.

Charles Schuster, President
Francisco Saa, Vice President, Marketing & Development
ARROWHEAD DISTRIBUTORS

Dedicated to my wife Gretchen whose intimate friendship, unwavering support, and unselfish love have enriched my life for almost a quarter century. Her special gifts and insights, so different than my own, have taught me from experience that one plus one can be much greater than two... the central message in this book.

TABLE OF CONTENTS

Preface

A central premise of today's more participatory leadership is that "all of us are smarter than any one of us." That certainly applies to the trends, concepts, and proposed actions recommended in this book. Its contents have evolved from over two years of strategic discussions encompassing the input of industry leaders within NACS, CSREF, NACSCORP, state and regional associations, private and contract management firms, and many individual members. Our goal here is to bring it all together into one simple, powerful, and actionable package.

From these discussions, we found that very few doubt that our industry is at a "Turning Point." The future will not be like the past. 'Business as usual' is no longer an option. A revolution in information technologies, combined with a fundamental shift in the way we organize work processes, is creating a new and much more competitive marketplace. Our members seem to know that. Most would have no qualms applying the words often attributed to Robert Kennedy: "If not now then when? If not us, then who?" They simply seek support in figuring out what to do. That's exactly what this book is intended to provide: a guide to developing a personal list of strategic things 'to do' to get ready.

Many years ago, futurist John Naisbitt predicted a world that would be both "high tech" and "high touch." That future has arrived. As business leaders, we must now sort out how to get "teleconnected" to both those we serve, and those we serve with, in ways that allow us to enhance operating efficiency and to personalize, customize, and target our interaction with customers. In effect, "high tech" enables "high touch."

The concept of Connections proposed in this book is intended to provide a simple, yet powerful planning framework. It suggests that the key to competitive advantage is to become intimately connected to customers to understand and respond to their needs in ways that far exceed the present norms of our industry. That's going to be a big job! Too big, in fact, for even the largest store or company. That's why the model goes on to suggest that we get connected to others who share common business interests in achieving it.

The core of this book are chapters two through six, which explain the concepts of understanding change and connecting to customers, campus partners, vendors, and coworkers. At the end of each chapter are three sets of resources:

- **Self assessment.** Use these charts to rank how important an objective is for your particular situation, how satisfied you are with your performance, and then calculate the "gap."
- **Store initiatives.** Select examples from these lists of things you can do, at your own store, to reinforce your work in the areas where you found the largest gaps.
- **Support from NACS.** Find background information and advice in the lists of materials and programs that NACS provides to assist your store in carrying out such initiatives you have chosen.

We hope you'll pause just long enough to develop a short list of what *you* will do to get better connected.

Further support of the Connections strategy:

At many of the state and regional association meetings in 1994 there will be presentations on ways to use the Connections strategy, the self-assessment tools, and the suggested store initiatives to help you plan for your own business. A workbook is also available for use by groups, or by individuals, to help in determining which aspects of the strategy you might want to begin working on. The workbook is a tool to help you brainstorm, prioritize, and then set basic 'to do' items on your calendars.

While these ideas and recommendations had to be captured at a certain point in time in order to produce the book you hold in your hand, it is our hope that Connections will always be evolving – a work in progress. Soon these materials will be available on the Internet, which will allow us to update them continuously as new ideas emerge. Your input is crucial to continuing the development of the Connections strategy, so we welcome your comments and suggestions.

We've also established a support center for Connections at NACS. If you have questions, or want information on materials that are available, please send e-mail to: CONNECTIONS@NACS.ORG

As Louis Pasteur once said, "chance favors only the prepared mind." While having a plan to succeed does not guarantee success, it certainly will change the odds. It's equally certain in these turbulent times that "failure to plan is planning to fail." Our overriding goal in the years ahead is to support your efforts to get ready for the most exciting opportunities our industry has ever seen.

Richard W. McDaniel, CSP
Ithaca, New York
August 1994

CHAPTER 1
CONNECTIONS:
NACS and YOU

Connecting NACS Members... Few words evoke deeper emotion or more aptly express what is special about our industry than "networking." It is the primary reason NACS was founded in 1923. Since that time, many life-long friendships have grown from the free and open exchange of ideas, insights, and skills among non-competing volunteers seeking to help each other. Many worry that the changes on the horizon may cause us to lose the special bond that connects our members. Yet, times have already changed. The pace is faster today and expectations are higher. Intensifying competition both inside and outside the membership leave members more hesitant to share "proprietary" ideas and noticeably more results-oriented when that sharing is deemed appropriate.

Yet, I deeply believe that these new conditions should be drawing us closer, not driving us apart. In many respects, the NACS tradition of bringing members together around common interests is even more valuable today; it's just that the old methods of networking are no longer adequate. The way we connect must change if we are to flourish under these new circumstances. Here are some observations:

- **Connections among members must become more results-oriented.** Just talking about issues won't suffice.

- **Connections must be more targeted.** There isn't enough time to do everything, only to do the most important things. This may mean that you'll want to connect to certain segments or individuals within the membership and consciously exclude others. For example, you may choose to participate in a financial survey that compares your store only to a set of mutually approved stores.

- **Connections must yield faster results.** Waiting until the next meeting may often be too little, too late.

- **Connections must be built upon more than information sharing.** They will include substantive co-development projects and real business partnerships.

The fact that a shared business purpose is our reason for connecting does not mean that our interactions will be less personal. To the contrary, co-development projects, strategic alliances, and joint ventures could actually draw us even closer, making partners of us, not just colleagues.

NACS Leadership Focus. It's hard to describe today's changing educational environment, much less our changing role in serving it. The

> *"The fact that a shared business purpose is our reason for connecting does not mean that our interactions will be less personal. To the contrary, co-development projects, strategic alliances, and joint ventures could actually draw us even closer, making partners of us, not just colleagues."*

complexity of the marketplace, regulation, and shifting competitive forces leave most of us perplexed, confused, anxious, and uncertain. Few industry leaders would dispute predictions of far-reaching changes to occur during this decade, yet most college store managers feel unprepared. That is the purpose of this "information package." **My vision of NACS leadership is to go beyond sounding an alarm and beyond simply citing major trends; it is to help stores identify and implement strategic initiatives—those vital tasks we**

must accomplish today on our campuses in order to compete
better tomorrow.

While there is no "one size fits all" strategy, today more than ever,
"failure to plan is planning to fail." Every college store, every
publisher, every supplier... indeed, everyone with a major stake in the
future of this industry, must hold fast to the helm, for we have already
entered turbulent times.

At first blush, this mandate to change may appear somewhat gloomy.
Nothing could be less true! There are few professional pursuits
worthier than implementing initiatives that enable people to learn. If
traditional products and methods must decline in the process, so be it.
We face unprecedented opportunities to introduce new products and
methods that will dramatically improve the efficiency and effectiveness
of education, and to redefine our own roles in the process.

No single entity, regardless of size, can go it alone. I am convinced
that we are entering a new era where targeted partnerships, coalitions,
and strategic alliances, occasionally even among competitors, must be
embraced in order to foster experimentation and rapid learning. If
IBM and Apple, or Toyota and GM can join hands at points of
common enterprise, perhaps retail stores can, too... large and small,
public and private, contracted and institutional. **Our goal must be to
pursue synergy through collaboration on issues of common concern
where we are not in competition, in order to foster an overall
competitive advantage.** One plus one can be greater than two.

Therefore, it is the central premise of this book that our success in the
'90s will increasingly require that we become "connected" to the
world we serve — to the people we serve and serve with, be they
customers, colleagues on campus, vendor representatives, or our own
coworkers. The material to follow is organized by this philosophical
framework, and suggests goals and strategies to help you forge those
vital connections.

Also described within the Connections framework are many NACS resources which support the membership in accomplishing local initiatives. In this way we hope to leverage NACS' historic role in facilitating strategic changes in the industry, through its products and services; through committees and task forces; through its foundation (CSREF) and distribution company (NACSCORP).

A more comprehensive companion piece, a hypermedia product, is under development. Because of its non-linear format, users may navigate the material in ways that best suit their particular interests. This companion piece demonstrates the value added by the very technologies discussed here. Soon it may even be posted as a free resource on the information superhighway, the Internet. The goal is to demonstrate in word and deed both the technical and human innovations being discussed and advocated.

... **"our success in the '90s will increasingly require that we become connected to the world we serve - - to the people we serve and serve with, be they customers, colleagues on campus, vendor representatives, or our own coworkers."**

CHAPTER 2
CHANGE IS NOT
WHAT IT USED TO BE

Our changing market. Even though traditional books account for almost two-thirds of today's net sales, it would be a grave mistake to conclude that we are in the "book" business. Our purpose, broader and more dynamic, is to accommodate the changing needs of faculty, staff, students, alumni, and campus visitors by providing products and services. Whether they be information products, insignia merchandise, or candy bars, our role on campus should be driven by our customers' needs.

Their needs are changing. The data is clear: students are busier, older, more diverse, and more computer literate, but less "book" literate. The faculty are younger, more diverse, under increasing pressure, and more computer literate. College administrators are under increasing fiscal pressure, and notably more business oriented. Alumni increasingly expect better stewardship from their alma maters as a condition for giving.

> *"In effect, the mandate to do more with less pervades both the teaching and support functions on nearly every campus in America, and the future promises much more of the same."*

And all these groups are more demanding. In effect, the mandate to do more with less pervades both the teaching and support functions on nearly every campus in America, and the future promises much more of the same.

The teaching materials are changing. It has been said that every cloud has a silver lining. In this instance, the silver lining is unmistakably the application of new information technologies to the teaching, research, and support functions integral to academe.

Computer costs continue to drop by almost half every two years while capabilities double, making applications cost-effective that would have seemed incredible only a few years before. We are building systems that act more and more like people. The "digitization of the universe" of text, sound, and video will ultimately result in new educational products that promise to initially supplement and eventually cannibalize the market for traditional textbooks. No one disputes this claim; we only debate the timetable.

Add to this the explosive growth of networks that connect computers and other supporting technologies. Collectively, they promise to eventually make both the location of computers and the way they work almost invisible to us. The more complicated and sophisticated systems get, the easier they are to use. The implication is clear... our world, our marketplace, is going to change even faster. The next round of change will eventually redefine "course materials" themselves and the way they are distributed.

> **"The 'digitization of the universe' of text, sound, and video will ultimately result in new educational products that promise to initially supplement and eventually cannibalize the market for traditional textbooks. No one disputes this claim; we only debate the timetables."**

The competition is changing. Alone, neither more demanding customers nor the existence of new technologies to serve them, causes change. Ultimately, it is competition that most dramatically impacts the rate of change on any given campus. This is particularly significant for college stores. Historically, many have believed we served a somewhat "captive market": faculty require texts, the store provides them, and students have no choice in the matter. Yet, in today's world, no market can be held hostage indefinitely.

Competition for control over sales on campus is intensifying. A substantial increase in the number of private stores is already underway, and contract management also continues an impressive growth trend expected to average 60 or more stores each year throughout the '90s. Yet, to focus exclusively on the traditional competitive scene may prove to be fatal. The most threatening competitors are even now entering our campus through the back door. Their collective activities promise to erode our business in small, sometimes imperceptible, increments:

- **Discounters and category killers.** Depending upon location and product mix, many stores are seeing much more aggressive behavior from traditional discounters such as Walmart or K-Mart, as well as innovative new discount retailers, including category killers, superstores, and warehouse stores. Their collective efforts siphon sales in supplies, trade books, and computer products.

- **Catalog sales.** Catalogs and 800 number services of all sorts are also permeating campuses, often offering next-day shipping, competitive pricing, and excellent selection and service.

- **Student price resistance.** Increasing numbers of students are creating their own alternatives to purchasing course materials from their college store because of the low perceived value of textbooks. Examples include:
    - Delaying the purchase of a book until they are sure it will be necessary to get a good grade

11

- Using copies found in libraries, or borrowed from friends

- Using campus networks to foster and streamline used book exchanges

• **Technology-based competitors.** The single most challenging long-term trend for college stores is the introduction of new technology-based teaching materials. Early entries include computer hardware and software, electronic custom publishing, and CD-ROM products. Because these digital products threaten to eventually cannibalize the traditional textbook business, forfeiture of this opportunity to computer labs, local computer stores, copy shops, or even the campus library will, in the end, prove disastrous. During the next three to seven years, the cumulative impact of these encroachments upon our core markets may be severe unless campus stores prepare now to sell and use these technologies.

Too often, discussions about the future degrade into pontifications about the promise of technology. The truth of the matter is that our future depends far more on people than on technology. The need for innovation has never been greater, and innovation is a uniquely human process. We, the people who serve this industry, must redefine our roles and reengineer our services if we are to successfully navigate this transition.

The primary argument advanced in this book is simple: if we are to compete in this increasingly fast-paced and demanding environment, we absolutely must invest part of today's efforts preparing for tomorrow. The focus of that preparation must be an uncompromising commitment to people: connecting to our customers, to our campus colleagues, to key vendor representatives, and to our own coworkers in innovative, synergistic, and results-oriented alliances that create competitive advantage.

"... if we are to compete in this increasingly fast-paced and demanding environment, we absolutely must invest part of today's efforts preparing for tomorrow. The focus of that preparation must be an uncompromising commitment to people: connecting to our customers, to our campus colleagues, to key vendor representatives, and to our own coworkers in innovative, synergistic, and results-oriented alliances that create competitive advantage."

Store Initiatives For Understanding Change

1. Collect campus plans.

College stores aren't alone in recognizing the need to plan and implement campus initiatives. Begin to collect strategic plans and/or goals and objectives from other units on campus, being sure to include:

- Institution's Planning Office
- Library
- Deans and Faculty
- The Development Office
- Academic Computing
- Information Technology Department
- Admissions and Registrar Offices
- Print Shop
- Physical Plant

Learn everything you can about what is being planned by others for your campus and the anticipated needs and perspectives of its various units. Ask colleagues from other college stores and vendors serving the market, to share their planning documents.

2. Collect local plans.

Contact your local Chamber of Commerce to obtain information about the business outlook for the local community. Look for population changes, possible new competitors, and the overall health of the local economy.

3. Keep up with industry trends.

Read the NACS Strategic Focus Summary (Appendix I of this book). Study the trends section and clearly articulate those changes you feel are most germane to your campus.

- To keep up with the changing world of academia, subscribe to the *Chronicle of Higher Education*, a "must read" for anyone involved in our industry.

Store Initiatives
For Understanding Change

- To stay abreast of technology used on your campus, subscribe to one or two magazines or newsletters, such as *MacUser* or *MacWorld, InfoWorld,* the *EDUCOM Review, Syllabus* or *PC World.*

4. Use the *"Wake-up Call."*

Find and review the "Industry Wake-up Call" package of two books, *Turning Points: Six Critical Challenges For College Stores* by Gary Shapiro and *The 1990's College Store Leadership Challenge: Achieving Excellence Through People* by Jeff Hallett, and the video *You Can Make A Difference,* which were distributed to every college store.

5. Identify initiatives.

As you work your way through the next few chapters, identify specific strategic initiatives, things you can do, that fit your circumstances. These initiatives will provide the basis for your own plan.

15

NACS SUPPORT

Publications:

- In addition to the Strategic Focus Summary and "Industry Wake-up Call," NACS recently published *College Store Planning: A Mission and Vision Kit* , which is an excellent planning tool.

- The NACS Industry Information and Research Department can advise on the best publications to read corresponding to your interest and the type(s) of computers used on campus.

Committees:

A number of important projects are being developed in this area by NACS committees, including:

- Identifying the new "core competencies" required for college stores to serve their campuses in the '90s (Certification)

- Creating a workshop on Mission and Vision (Professional Development)

See the appendix for more details.

CHAPTER 3 CUSTOMER CONNECTIONS

A tradition of isolation from customers. In his recent book, *The Only Thing That Really Matters*, Karl Albrecht argues that ultimately the key factor in today's business is consistently delivering what customers value. This is hardly a controversial insight. How can anyone hope to succeed without knowing and delivering what customers perceive to be of value? Yet, college stores, publishers, and vendors know surprisingly little about our customers. What we do know indicates an alarming level of customer dissatisfaction with our core products and services, which we all too often dismiss or rationalize as attributable to "institutional stigma," "industry-wide misconceptions," or just "unrealistic customer expectations." An example is the widespread view that campus stores deliberately charge exorbitant markups, especially on textbooks, in order to take advantage of students in a captive market.

Even now, new competitors are at the doorstep whispering appealing messages to our students, faculty, staff, alumni, and campus visitors. Why not… "buy your software by catalog," "visit the discount store on your way to campus," or "use the library and save your money?" Many more are on the way. Connecting to our customers, understanding and acting upon their perceptions about what has value and how well we're delivering it, is no longer optional… it is the price of entry.

The product: customers value getting what they came for. Whether your point of reference is the latest research or just common sense, nothing is more important to a customer than reliably getting what they came for in terms of quality, selection, and price. For most stores in our industry, that currently means:

1. Academic Products	Textbooks, trade books, supplies, and computer products
2. Specialty Products	Emblematic gifts and clothing
3. Convenience Products	Ranging from snacks to film

While it may be obvious, it's worth noting that this list has been prioritized both with regard to the typical store's sales figures and its mission on campus. Clearly, providing academic products is the life blood of our industry. What may be less obvious, especially on smaller campuses, is that the products our customers need and value are already changing, and nowhere will this change be more pervasive than for academic products. This is essentially due to a quiet revolution underway, which is developing impressive new teaching tools and enhancing the old ones. Computer costs drop by half every two years as their capabilities double, networks that link them together proliferate, and there is no end in sight to these developments.

"Connecting to our customers, understanding and acting upon their perceptions about what has value and how well we're doing at delivering it, is no longer optional... it is the price of entry."

Traditional textbooks will have more and more competition as this smorgasbord of teaching tools is expanded to encompass more exotic and specialized options. No one debates the trends described here and no one denies that they will ultimately pervade the college store industry. Instead, the debate centers on how fast they will come.

Most argue that the impact will be significant in this decade. If your customers value getting all their academic products at your "information store," can anyone long ignore their growing demand for digital products such as software, CD-ROM-based tutorials, or customized products? So what must you do?

Strategy and product life cycle. (See illustration on following page.) Few products last forever. They tend to be improved, replaced over time, or subjected to so much competition that prices and profits decline. This reality is reflected in an old, but useful marketing model called the product life cycle.

When a product is introduced, sales develop slowly as the bugs are worked out and people become familiar with it. When it catches on, sales grow rapidly. Eventually, however, sales flatten as new competitors come along and the market matures. Finally, sales and profits decline as competition intensifies still further and new products are introduced that supersede it.

Consider this in the context of the major products currently sold in the college store. At what stage are traditional textbooks, trade books, supplies, soft goods, or convenience merchandise? The answer might unnerve you.

An Industry Facing Decline

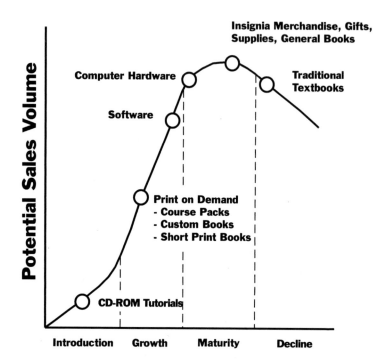

The inescapable conclusion is that most of the mainstream products we sell today are in the mature to declining stage of the cycle. Unless we both adopt new products and reenergize the old ones by adding value, sales and profits will decline.

What to do during introduction and growth: "Get started!" As promising new academic products come to the marketplace, learn about them, find ways to use them, and whenever possible, begin selling them. Today, almost every store should be aware of, and involved in distributing, custom publishing (course packets), computer hardware and software, and CD-ROM tutorials. Where there are market or political constraints, find creative ways to get involved by partnering with others on and off campus (even with competitors where necessary) so that your operation has a toe in the water. Make a way to become involved. Failure to do so may be scarcely noticed next year, but eventually it could threaten your existence on campus.

General College Store Industry Sales

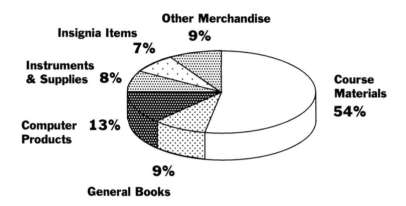

Source: *1994 NACS Annual Financial Survey*, p. 9.

Compare the above chart showing industry-wide sales to your product mix. Most stores will conclude that significant sales revenues have already been lost to competitors. Of greater concern is the probability that these lost revenues represent the new technology-based/ customized products.

What to do during maturity and decline: "Add value." Without intervention on your part, competition will intensify, and sales and profits will atrophy. Yet there are still tremendous opportunities for those who are connected to their customers and understand how to add value in their eyes. Value can be added by making core products more convenient, refining systems and procedures, improving service quality, or improving the design of your facilities. The next section will offer more specific suggestions.

Store Initiatives
To Meet Product Needs

1. New product assessment and adoption.

Meet with the people involved in academic computing, computer lab(s), and campus media/technology support.

- Ask them to identify faculty/departments using new technology in their teaching. Ask about CD-ROM use on campus.

- Ask about campus-wide technology plans.

Meet with the campus print shop to find out which departments are the greatest users of classroom handouts. Ask the library reserve room if they are interested in having the store print and sell some of the materials that are placed on reserve and are photocopied anyway by students.

2. Reduce "high price" image.

Identify and implement steps designed to reduce the problem of your store's high price image on campus. Consider ways to position your store as the advocate of the student to insure that they conveniently get the course materials they need, on time, and at a price they perceive as reasonable.

- Meet with the editor of the campus newspaper and the head of the student government. Review your policies regarding textbook prices to prevent them from becoming an issue on campus.

3. Custom publishing.

Become more aggressive in developing or expanding your custom publishing business, encouraging the use of custom publishing by faculty.

- Develop a marketing campaign to faculty and their departments to funnel this business through your store rather than through off-campus copy shops.

- Develop relationships and negotiate prices with a variety of printing and production centers.

Store Initiatives
To Meet Product Needs

4. Computer hardware sales.

Reexamine your store's role in technology sales, and decide on a desired vision for hardware sales if the sales environment changes.

- Partnerships between academic computing, (other) campus computer resellers, and the college store are vital.

NACS SUPPORT:

Services and Projects:

- **CCPSS.** The NACS Copyright and Custom Publishing Support Service (CCPSS) offers advice, materials and services of value in starting or enhancing your custom publishing business, including a *Custom Publishing Background Kit.*

- **Copyright permissions preapproval.** NACS is actively facilitating the development and implementation of technology-based preapproval models for acquiring and granting copyright permission. This process will reduce costs, streamline processes, and speed delivery of custom-published products through the creation of open and flexible standards which accommodate diverse rights holder and user requirements.

- **Teaching Materials of the Future.** (TMOTF) This project being conducted by the American Association for Higher Education (AAHE) and cosponsored by NACS, provides a number of interesting insights into the changing educational product. The primary goal of the TMOTF project is to help understand, shape, and smooth the transition to new systems for developing, publishing, distributing, and using materials - both print and electronic - that will support better teaching and learning in higher education. Many of the insights are being communicated via a listserv (e-mail discussion list), which college stores can join by sending e-mail to: listserv@gwuvm.gwu.edu, with the message: subscribe aahesgit yourfirstname yourlastname.

- **NACSCORP** is an excellent resource for information on software and CD-ROM products.

Professional Development:

NACS has a variety of professional development opportunities in the world of changing products:

24

NACS SUPPORT:

- Custom publishing programs are offered in conjunction with most NACS events, either as stand-alone seminars, or as concentrations within other conferences.

- The annual Summer Institute offers value-added sessions on selling technology products.

- The first annual Conference on Textbooks and Technology (ConTEXT), an advanced program related to both today's and tomorrow's issues in selling course materials, is planned for Winter of 1995.

- New product technology will be a major emphasis of the NACS Annual Meeting in St. Louis in April, 1995.

Committees:

A variety of new initiatives in this area are taking place under the direction of NACS committees, specifically:

- Understanding, identifying, and inventing successful practices to reverse the "high price" image of college stores (Textbook Perceptions Task Force)
- Creating a campus technology assessment project (Textbook/Course Materials)
- Preparing a briefing kit for campus newspapers on textbook prices (Textbook/Course Materials)
- Identifying what college stores can learn from the use of technology in the health science field (Health Science Stores)
- Developing models to help stores promote environmental programs, so that they will be acknowledged on campus as leading/participating in environmental efforts (Environmental Concerns)

See the appendix for more details.

Customers value a "legendary" experience. Successfully delivering the products and services that customers come in for, even the new ones, will not make us heroes on campus. Customers expect it. After all, that's what campus stores were created to do. The greatest opportunity for outstanding business performance today involves consciously seeking to do more than customers expect. In recent years, this notion has been popularized by well-known author, Dr. Kenneth Blanchard under the label "Legendary Service"... service so good that it makes "raving fans" of customers, as described in his book of the same name. While at first blush this may sound a bit hokey, believe me, it's not! It is this legendary experience that can differentiate your store from all others in the minds of customers.

Exceeding expectations requires that we first understand what customers value, and then set about to deliver more of it. Four such elements are convenience, design, systems, and service. Thinking about how to add value by improving the customer experience is a great first step.

Customers experience convenience. Access to the store's core products and services at convenient times and locations adds value. Traditionally, this has prompted many stores to adopt changes such as longer hours, branch locations, and catalog ordering. Some of the more recent innovations to improve customer convenience include:

- **Shopping services.** Some stores offer students a service whereby their textbooks are picked and packed in advance of their arrival on campus, then picked up by the student at the store at the beginning of the term.

- **Express delivery.** A handful of stores are exploring expanded campus delivery services to offices and dorms, to be used by customers when "it absolutely, positively, has to get there."

- **The "transient store."** By putting store products in mobile sales fixtures, retail operations can actually be set up and dismantled whenever and wherever needed on campus for short bursts of

CUSTOMER VALUE

According to Karl Albrecht, *The Only Thing That Really Matters* is delivering total customer value. This illustration suggests that while the core element of value is the product itself, it is the customer experience of your store's design, systems, convenience, and service that adds beauty and fragrance...that makes you memorable.

retail activity. The concept encompasses everything from rush (textbook) sales at branch locations, to temporary setups to sell books on site at major lectures, or memorabilia just outside an important alumni event. This represents a powerful extension of retail service.

- **The teleconnected store.** By applying simple-to-use technology, it is now feasible to set up a small room teleconnected to a regional or campus headquarters, where customers can come and be linked visually to a service center. There, an operator/ receptionist with systems connections could provide expanded special order services in a very personal format. This concept could be applied on large campuses to stay in touch with outlying areas, on multi-campus universities, or at small schools to enable customers to access quality service while closing down operations between rushes.

- **Desktop services... "home shopping."** The basic concept is to enable any customer with a computer and modem (from an office, dorm room, or anywhere) to access store services for inquiry and ordering. This will become popular on leading campuses by the end of this decade.

Note that none of these innovations changes the product! Yet, they all add value to the customer by making existing products more convenient and accessible.

Customers experience design. Customers also value elements of the facilities design. Without saying so, they routinely appraise how clean, attractive, and easy-to-use our facilities are. However today, clean, attractive, and easy-to-use facilities are considered basic. That's why many schools have moved on to design fun, exciting, interesting, and/or specialized environments. Some innovative examples include:

- **Targeted merchandising concepts.** Some larger schools have constructed "collegiate shopping malls" featuring a collection of specialty niches targeted to different elements of campus life and activity. Others have achieved a department store look. Still others have created specialty shops, or a particular feel to their merchandising spaces, which are uniquely suited to their campuses. This concept could be used at some level by virtually any store.

- **Cultural synchronization.** Another innovation is to synchronize merchandising, design, and promotion to campus life by using pictures and graphics depicting campus scenes or logos in interesting ways. Some stores use promotions that go well beyond traditional author signings by tying into major events on campus, such as employee day, finals week, or important lecture series.

- **Floating spaces.** While some bemoan the inadequacy of sales space, others have literally built their stores on wheels, or purchased flexible fixturing. These innovations allow radical shifts of existing space four to six times a year, designed to service different market opportunities during nonrush cycles. This is an incredibly powerful, though rare, technique that can yield sales per square foot results of two to five times industry norms.

Customers experience our systems. The broadest definition of systems encompasses policies, procedures, processes, and equipment. Together, they dramatically affect what our customers think of us. Imagine the composite effect of long checkout lines, an offensive or unreasonable refund policy, and incomprehensible buyback procedures. Now look around your store. These and other equally damaging systems deficiencies are commonplace among college stores even today, when customer expectations are rising rapidly. Some trends and innovations in this area include:

- **POS, EFT, UPC, PLU, EIEIO.** If you can see past the barrage of acronyms and technical jargon, you'll find that a major innovation today is the widespread adoption of electronic check-out devices that save money and serve customers much faster. These point-of-sale (POS) registers typically feature electronic funds transfers (EFT) of bankcard collections, and can potentially eliminate most ticketing costs by using manufacturer's bar codes, i.e., universal product codes (UPC) and price look up (PLUs) on the registers. The bottom line is this...

Easy checkout
Increased customer information
Enhanced efficiency/lower operating costs
Increased management information
On-line access to bank and store inventory systems

Times have changed, benefits have increased, and costs have remained constant or declined. Most stores of a half million or more in sales volume should reconsider POS.

- **Buying systems.** While it's no longer a cutting edge application, buying systems are also proliferating, often featuring specialized modules for textbooks, trade books, general merchandise, and accounting. This, too, is worth considering. Stores of nearly any size can cost-justify a textbook module and PUBNET today.

- **Systems integration.** The single most significant innovation in recent years is systems integration, i.e., connecting store systems directly to other stores, to the campus, to banking systems, and to vendors.

Customers experience our service. Whether your employees are surly or apathetic, or caring and thoughtful has a tremendous impact on the customer experience. That's why knowledgeable, friendly, efficient, responsive staff increasingly constitute the most crucial difference between retail winners and losers. Examples of current innovations include:

- **The professionalization of service delivery.** One of the most significant changes in this area is the movement to empower front-line staff to manage day-to-day service delivery functions. This is accomplished by broadening their job descriptions and decision-making authority to encompass the routine monitoring and continuous improvement of service quality.

- **Field rep system.** As products become more varied, complex, and customized, there is a growing demand for staff in the field to work with key faculty and administrators to provide an expanded set of specialized services ranging from "curriculum consulting" to client-selling.

SELF ASSESSMENT

CUSTOMER CONNECTIONS	A Importance	B Satisfaction	A - B = G Gap
Feedback Systems - Knowing what customers really value and how well your store is delivering it. (*Examples: Comment cards, focus groups, periodic customer surveys.*)	1 2 3 4 5 6 7	1 2 3 4 5 6 7	☐ - ☐ = ☐
New Products - Delivering the types of new teaching materials my campus needs. (*Examples: Computer hardware and software, CD-ROM tutorials, custom course packs.*)	1 2 3 4 5 6 7	1 2 3 4 5 6 7	☐ - ☐ = ☐
Convenience - Making products and services easier for customers to access. (*Examples: Pre-packaging textbooks, catalog/delivery services, special sales at remote locations.*)	1 2 3 4 5 6 7	1 2 3 4 5 6 7	☐ - ☐ = ☐
Store Design - Making store facilities easier to navigate and aesthetically appealing. (*Example: Signage, attractive displays, flexible use of space.*)	1 2 3 4 5 6 7	1 2 3 4 5 6 7	☐ - ☐ = ☐
System/Procedures - Making store systems and procedures serve customers better. (*Examples: POS, computerized product management, customer-friendly policies and procedures.*)	1 2 3 4 5 6 7	1 2 3 4 5 6 7	☐ - ☐ = ☐
Service Standards - Defining standards to ensure knowledgeable, friendly, efficient and responsive service. (*Examples: Eye contact, offering help within 60 seconds; diversity training.*)	1 2 3 4 5 6 7	1 2 3 4 5 6 7	☐ - ☐ = ☐

Store Initiatives
For Customer Experience:

1. Monitoring what customers value.

Dramatically increase your understanding of what your customers value. Implement a comprehensive customer feedback system including surveys, focus groups, and comment cards to monitor your customers' perceptions about what has value and how successful your store is delivering it.

2. Customer roundtables.

Hold at least three brainstorming/roundtable discussions with groups of customers to listen to their ideas about your products and services, and how you can better support them.

- Consider forming a customer board of advisors to give you regular feedback from a customer perspective, and to act as store advocates on campus.

3. Convenience innovations.

Consider what steps can be taken to make your stores' products and services more convenient to your customers. Include longer hours, temporary and remote setups, and even desktop ordering (if appropriate).

For each, specify in detail what it is that you would propose to do, who will be in charge, and when the project should be completed.

4. Physical design innovations.

If your store hasn't been substantially renovated in several years, consider developing a renovation plan to maximize use of space, improve traffic flow, provide better access for the physcially challenged, and improve signage and check-out space.

Store Initiatives
For Customer Experience:

- Consider redesigning your store around flexible space. Use moveable fixtures, and rearrange your space before and after book rush.

- If a major renovation is impossible, consider a smaller project. Turn some or all of your store's textbook space into multipurpose sales space during non-rush sales periods. Examine your aisle location, signage, lighting, and decor, and compare them to places that attract today's students.

5. Systems and procedures innovations.

Make systems, policies, and procedures more customer-friendly. Consider investing in PUBNET, textbook management, POS and other systems.

6. Service innovations.

Use customer feedback to identify ways to improve the quality of the relationships between your customers and your staff. Emphasize the importance of training and ongoing feedback on key staff attributes (i.e. friendliness, knowledge, efficiency, and responsiveness).

NACS SUPPORT

Publications:

- The NACS *College Store Service Quality Research Kit,* developed by Stephen McDaniel, PhD of the Center For Retailing Studies at Texas A&M University with the support of CSREF through a grant from John Marcus, CSP and Matthews Medical/CBA Bookstores, is an excellent tool which includes surveys and analysis methods to determine if your store meets the service expectations of your customers.

- NACS also has a *College Store Service Quality Surveys Background Information Kit* containing samples of store-designed quality service surveys.

- *Service Quality Means Survival For Your Store* is a monograph and video of a presentation made by Dr. Leonard Berry of Texas A&M which illustrates how college stores can deliver outstanding service.

- The NACS *Considerations in College Store Renovation and Design* is a book to help college stores create retail spaces that deliver on customer expectations.

Professional Development:

- The NACS Merchandising Center offers a variety of videos from CareerTrack and other organizations that provide employee training in customer service and sales.

Committees:

- Establishing customer service benchmarks and good practices (College Store Evaluation and the new Successful Practices and Benchmarks Task Force, first established in 1994-1995)

NACS SUPPORT

- Setting industry benchmarks for effective use of space and serving customers in remote locations (Merchandising)

- Identifying national student demographic trends and the needs of groups such as distance learners, life-long learners, and older students (Community/Junior/ Technical College Stores)

- Identifying product and service issues for specific cultural and ethnic groups on campus (Cultural Diversity)

See the appendix for more details.

CHAPTER 4
CAMPUS
CONNECTIONS

A tradition of isolation from campus. When asked to characterize the typical administrator's view of the college store during a 1990 CSREF Forum on "The Future of the Institutional College Store," Bob Golden, VP of Business and Finance at Bowie State University, was succinct. Frankly, he said, "we hardly know you're there." Stores tend to quietly and anonymously go about their business. Bob went on to suggest that this is usually considered to be okay because administrators want "no hassles" from their stores, anyway. Complaints from disgruntled faculty, students, alumni, and campus officials are anathema to the administrator. In effect, no news is good news. Finally, he smiled and said, "Oh, by the way — we also need more money." No one in the audience disagreed.

At the 1990 NACS Collegiate Retailing Symposium, "An Industry in Transition: Academic Products In The 1990s," there was discussion about the future of educational products. There, Dr. Russell Adams summarized the academic's view of the college store with the words "book butlers." He meant that faculty view the store's role as mechanical and mundane, not substantive and collaborative. Bookstores serve by ordering, receiving, shelving, selling, and returning textbooks... nothing more, nothing less.

These images portray the typical "bookstore" as operating at arm's length from other college functions, both administrative and academic. Most store managers have historically seen themselves more as "retailers" and "business people" than "administrators" or "academics." Many have been quite comfortable running good businesses with only the most cursory links to their colleges.

Finding a fit. Technological developments and other forces are already beginning to impact the tools and methods of teaching at most colleges. In effect, the cards are in the air all at once, and there will soon be a new deal. However, unlike a card game, we can substantially influence our own hand if we act soon.

Never has there been a greater need for college stores to fundamentally rethink our role in serving the campus. Many believe that "distributing information products" will require a much more integral link to the teaching and research functions of the institution than "selling textbooks." Faculty will need special assistance in identifying the right resources from a growing body of information, customizing their course materials, and communicating the core content to students. Whether college stores are able to step into this role depends a great deal on what we do in the next few years. Only in the light of a shared, campus-wide vision can one effectively begin to develop one's full potential.

"By forging connections to the library, faculty, administrators, university press, print shop, information technologies department, and other campus entities, every store can be in the loop, a key partner in the most significant change this industry has ever seen."

Therefore, each college store must "find a fit," uniquely matching its strengths to the college's broader purposes. Because the strengths of stores vary, as do institutional purposes, there is no universal solution. However, a store without a plan to effectively contribute to key campus initiatives will, in all probability, find itself downsizing its operations in just a few years. Here are four possible outlets for integrating our stores:

1. Information products and services: Books are linear information packages. They will not go away in the next decade. However, they are already being supplemented by many new information formats. Software, custom publishing (soon electronic custom publishing) and CD-ROM products are too important to ignore. It's hard to imagine a successful college store in the year 2000 that is not involved in the distribution of these products, or those that may supersede them.

It is not necessary that every store sell all information products. What is necessary is that every successful store be a part of a campus-wide partnership that effectively supplies students and faculty with the information products they need. In other words, you don't have to do it alone. By forging connections to the library, faculty, administrators, university press, print shop, information technologies department, and other campus entities, every store can be in the loop, a key partner in the most significant change this industry has ever seen. Examples of other initiatives to expand your store's personal outreach to campus include:

- **Curriculum consulting.** Offer key faculty, such as those teaching very large classes, an expanded set of services for planning their class materials, including custom publishing, special supplies, and presentation aids. Becoming knowledgeable in pedagogical techniques that help academics get their ideas and insights across to students is also of potentially significant value to the campus of the future.

- **Technology fair.** Bring vendors or technology pioneers to campus to offer seminars and demonstrations to faculty.

Understanding, targeting, and integrating the store's information products and services to better meet the needs of other academic units on campus is one of the most strategic initiatives in which stores can be involved.

2. Public relations. It is often the case that, due to its prime location or other features, the store can make a substantial contribution to the college's mission by supporting public relations initiatives. Examples include:

- **Emblematic catalog or brochure services** providing alumni with access to memorabilia

- **Specialized selections of books and other academic products** highlighting important disciplines at your school

- **Special services** for campus visitors and conferences

Accomplishing these things effectively will typically require strong connections with other units on campus who share public relations responsibilities, including:
- Admissions
- Public Relations
- Development
- Alumni Services
- Summer Conferences

3. Business services. Because college stores are designed to efficiently conduct business transactions on a daily basis, they may collaborate with other administrative units on campus to become an outlet for other services. Examples include:

- Sale of athletic, theater, or other tickets

- Acting as an outlet for the cashier, bursar, admissions, or registrar's office for targeted types of transactions

4. Financial support. As colleges face increasing fiscal pressures, auxiliary services, including college stores, are expected to provide more direct financial support. Whether through contract management or independent operation, campus administrators often consciously seek a higher return on the various assets they commit to operating the store. (e.g. inventory, working capital, well-located buildings).

At the same time, local town-gown interactions frequently leave administrators hesitant to price "below the market" in order to avoid the appearance of "unfair competition." Within such a framework, unless a store is subsidizing services that the campus considers critical for nonfinancial reasons, it is logical to anticipate that a well run enterprise, pricing its products competitively, will generate a competitive profit. Failure to reach conscious consensus on this matter with their bosses will leave many store managers "surprised" in the years ahead.

The core insight is this: When stores operate in relative isolation, they fall far short of their potential to serve their campuses. Today's increasing demands cannot be satisfied by any one campus resource. Many partnerships are already forming on campus, and without effective campus connections they will not include, and at worst will be competitive with, the college store.

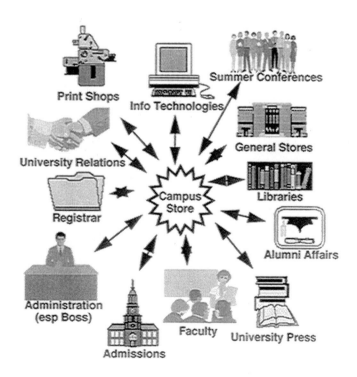

SELF ASSESSMENT

CAMPUS CONNECTIONS	A Importance	B Satisfaction	A - B = G Gap
Information Products- Collaborating with other campus units to develop, produce and distribute new information products *(Examples: Faculty, library, information technology department, print shop.)*	1 2 3 4 5 6 7	1 2 3 4 5 6 7	□ - □ = □
Public Relations - Collaborating with other campus units to improve the image of the college. *(Examples: PR office, development office, alumni affairs, human resources, admissions.)*	1 2 3 4 5 6 7	1 2 3 4 5 6 7	□ - □ = □
Financial Expectations - Developing consensus regarding store financial expectations. *(Examples: Your boss, budget/planning office, senior administrators.)*	1 2 3 4 5 6 7	1 2 3 4 5 6 7	□ - □ = □
Integrated Planning - Ensuring that store plans align with overall campus priorities. *(Examples: Your boss, budget/planning office, senior administrators.)*	1 2 3 4 5 6 7	1 2 3 4 5 6 7	□ - □ = □
Campus Teleconnections - Connecting your store to the campus network and the Internet. *(Examples: E-mail; desktop services e.g.... faculty adoptions; access store database via network, home/office shopping.)*	1 2 3 4 5 6 7	1 2 3 4 5 6 7	□ - □ = □
Campus Events - Collaborate with other units on planning/administration of major academic and social events. *(Examples: Author signings, remote sales to support special events.)*	1 2 3 4 5 6 7	1 2 3 4 5 6 7	□ - □ = □

Store Initiatives
For Campus Connections:

1. Faculty as client.

To define what faculty value in your store and to develop a strategy to respond to those needs, invite several groups of faculty to roundtables over lunch to brainstorm and discuss this issue. If you are uncomfortable in acting as moderator, request faculty from the Marketing Department or Business School to plan and conduct these events.

- Consider developing and offering Bookstore 101 to inform new faculty (and department assistants responsible for book orders) about the best ways to work with the store and learn about store services they might not otherwise discover.

- Pick one or two faculty teaching large classes, and meet with them to brainstorm ways your store can expand its services to them, including help with custom publishing.

2. A shared mission/vision.

Develop a shared vision and mission within your campus, involving the key stakeholders (e.g. your boss, the key faculty, and administrators). Define your role and reach consensus about both your role and the particular initiatives you are pursuing to advance it.

3. Develop a partnering strategy.

Understand the needs of others on campus as a context for developing partnerships. Use this framework for experimentation. An obvious starting point is to develop or join a campus partnership exploring new course materials.

4. Getting started.

In what ways will your store advance the overall campus mission? More specifically, how will you further:

Store Initiatives
For Campus Connections:

- The sale and distribution of information products and services
- Public relations
- Business services
- Financial support

Define your ideal role, one that reflects your best efforts to match your present and prospective strengths to the core purposes of your institution. Write it in summary form on a document of no more than three pages. For each planned connection, what specific actions will you take to advance it within the next two years? Be careful to specify who will lead the initiative. Review your plan to connect to campus with your boss to gain consensus and support. Then actively sell it and solicit feedback from other major campus stakeholders whose support and partnership is necessary for success.

5. Marketing.
Market the store as a vital part of the full educational mission of the campus, working to establish credibility as information experts.

- If your campus has an institutional computer store, discuss with them your approach to computer software sales, and where they might suggest you target your software sales activities.

- By regularly visiting departments, and by working with campus technology centers, find out which faculty are integrating applications software into their curriculum.

6. Electronic networks.
Connect your store to the campus network and the Internet.

Store Initiatives
For Campus Connections:

- Experiment with accepting and replying to electronic mail (i.e., textbook requisitions and/or inquiries) from faculty who are regular network users.

- Experiment with the use of databases, especially those available on campus and those available through commercial providers.

- Explore putting your store's textbook and/or other inventory database on a network for use by faculty and students.

7. Campus library.
Establish a relationship with the campus librarian to:

- Discover the degree to which the library is planning to initiate or expand the availability of electronically stored/distributed information to students and faculty.

- Develop an attitude of cooperation, looking for mutually beneficial opportunities and other ways to work together as campus information delivery changes.

NACS SUPPORT

Services and Projects:

- **Teaching Materials of the Future.** (TMOTF) This project being conducted by the American Association for Higher Education (AAHE), and co-sponsored by NACS, provides a number of interesting insights into the needs of faculty as they begin to adopt new course materials. (See page 24)

- **Electronic course reserves.** NACS has cosponsored two events with the Association for Research Libraries (ARL) to bring representatives from campus libraries and college stores together to discuss the implementation of electronic reserve functions. This built upon earlier ARL/NACS work to facilitate collaboration between libraries and college stores.

Publications:

- The NACS *College Store Planning: A Mission and Vision Kit* is an essential tool as you work to develop a shared mission/ vision on campus.

- *Links: Faculty, College Stores, Publishers and Students* is a valuable booklet to distribute on campus to help faculty understand the issues involved in providing their students with textbooks and other course materials.

- *College, Universities and Institutional Stores: Partners in Higher Education* is a NACS background kit examining the changing nature of the college store and how stores can become an integral part of campus life.

- The *NACS Annual Financial Survey* presents some of the data you need to develop financial goals for store operations.

NACS SUPPORT

Professional Development:

- NACS offers seminars on financial management and problem solving; and campus relations sections are included in both the College Store Operations and College Store Management seminars.

Committees:

- Helping stores connect to, and use, campus and other networks (Retail Systems Advisory, Institutional Stores/ Campus Relations, Smaller Stores, Professional Development)

- Identifying successful methods stores use to get campus consensus on mission and performance standards (Institutional Stores/Campus Relations)

- Understanding key issues and interests of potential campus partners (Institutional Stores/Campus Relations)

- Creating models to communicate customized financial performance information (Financial Survey)

- Identifying industry financial and service benchmarks (Financial Survey and Successful Practices and Benchmarks Task Force)

- Determining what faculty value from a college store (Textbooks/Course Materials)

- Outlining a new faculty orientation program for communicating textbook and college store issues (Textbooks/Course Materials)

- Creating workshops on mission and vision, campus relations, and working with bosses and other administrative personnel (Professional Development)

- Identifying successful alliances between college stores and microcenters (Campus Computer Resellers Alliance)

See the appendix for more details.

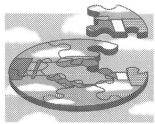

CHAPTER 5
VENDOR
CONNECTIONS

A tradition of isolation from corporate suppliers. In a sense, we weren't always isolated. Only a few years ago, a commonplace mode of interacting with suppliers was termed "relationship buying." By building a relationship with the buyer, vendor representatives could often effectively lock in an account. This might include special treatment, such as occasional favors, and frequent sales calls, often reflected in higher vendor costs to stores and higher prices to customers.

While some "relationship buying" remains, widespread expansion of contract management, category killers, discount stores, and other competitive options, coupled with increasing fiscal demands on stores from parent institutions, have prompted a very clear shift in the last half dozen years to "negotiated buying." This approach typically pits buyer representatives (buying groups) against vendors, resulting in more competitive buying and usually less personal service. It's much harder to compete today if a store cannot buy on a competitive basis. Typically, that requires buying more of fewer items from fewer companies.

Another promising trend is now on the rise in our industry. It involves results-oriented connections with a few larger suppliers, where both consciously embrace win-win strategic initiatives that either reduce the total cost of doing business together, or increase total revenue. This is accomplished by jointly focusing on successfully selling to the ultimate customer.

Joint efforts to reduce total costs. Note that the total cost of the vendor connection includes such categories as ordering, receiving, shelving, promotion, and returning. In the past, when a cost category was primarily the responsibility of the vendor, such as sales calls, store buyers had little interest or incentive to help control it. Similarly, if the cost category was primarily the responsibility of the store, such as receiving, the vendor was inclined to ignore it. When major suppliers work collaboratively with retailers, it is possible to reduce these costs and share the benefits. Examples include:

> **"It is finally becoming clear to many that reducing the costs incurred by both supplier and retailer are opportunities to both"**

- **Reducing receiving/ticketing costs.** It is possible to dramatically reduce the number of products ticketed by using "bin-pricing" and scanning vendor affixed bar codes at the point of sale. It's common today for retailers such as grocery or discount stores to work with suppliers to put machine-readable bar codes on their merchandise to uniquely identify each item. When stores have point-of-sale registers, and can also put the price on the shelf (rather than on the item), they can eliminate ticketing costs, process price changes faster, and both receive and return merchandise faster.

- **Preagreements.** Another major cost-cutting opportunity involves establishing permission preagreements to expedite and encourage the legal use of intellectual property. With the explosive growth of custom publishing, the problem of illegal photocopying has mushroomed. It is estimated that between three and six copies are illegally made for every one that is paid for. The primary reason seems to be that acquiring permission takes too long and requires too much labor. At the same time, publishers often waste most of the revenues received on inefficient and unwieldy manual approval systems. Because as many as 75% of the articles are reused from year to year, much of the time and labor are spent reauthorizing the same materials. By establishing preagreements and systematizing the request granting process, both publishers and retail outlets stand to gain substantially in increased revenues and decreased clearance costs.

- **Reducing the publisher returns percentage for textbook and trade book publishers.** Currently, approximately 22% of textbook purchases and 30% of general book purchases are returned to publishers and distributors. The cost of initial shipping and receiving, damages, and return shipping and receiving is substantial for both parties. It is clearly a matter of joint interest to identify methods and incentives to cut this expense.

- **Reducing freight costs.** Current estimates place total freight cost at between 2.5% and 3% of purchases. By working with suppliers, it is possible for stores to both negotiate much lower total costs charged by freight companies, and to consolidate receiving to a smaller number of shippers, thereby enhancing overall efficiency for stores.

Joint efforts to increase total revenues. When vendors focus on increasing their own short-term revenues without regard for the buyer's interests, stores typically end up overstocked. The results include overcrowded, poorly presented shelves, increased loss due to damage, obsolescence and pilferage and slow sell through rates. Naturally, the vendor receives much smaller reorders (if any). Amazingly, this is still a common scenario, driven perhaps in part by competitive pressures among vendors and inexperienced buying.

Once the issue of competitive buying has been settled, it is in the interest of both the store and the vendor/publisher to cooperate fully as partners in order to understand and sell to the ultimate customers: students, faculty, staff, alumni, and campus visitors. In fact, high stock turnover rates, attractive merchandising, good customer service, fair pricing, effective promotions, and all other typically "retail" concerns are as critical to suppliers as they are to stores. Unless these ultimate customers buy, there can be no second sale. Stated somewhat differently, whatever deficiencies exist in retailing activities will impact the vendor's pocketbook as negatively as it does the store's;

the reverse is also often true. This constitutes the business basis for a win-win connection. Examples of vendor involvement include:

- Improving point of purchase displays
- Developing and implementing creative promotion plans
- Selling on site during prime seasons
- Training store staff both in sales techniques and the product features
- Conducting targeted market research
- Refining buying systems to enable reliable just-in-time inventory
- Enhancing product security systems

The core principle is this: When college stores partner with a small number of core suppliers who offer competitive pricing programs, both parties can devote conscious efforts to providing the best possible products and services to the ultimate customer at the lowest possible operating costs. While most stores do engage in ad hoc, patchwork partnerships, few of us have really devoted the energy to define our partners and to develop deliberate plans to optimize our relationships. Those who do could garner significant competitive advantage in the years to come.

> **"When college stores partner with a small number of core suppliers who offer competitive pricing programs, both parties can devote conscious efforts to providing the best possible products and services to the ultimate customer at the lowest possible operating costs."**

SELF ASSESSMENT

VENDOR CONNECTIONS	A Importance	B Satisfaction	A - B = G Gap
Number of Vendors - Optimizing the number of vendors per product category. *(Examples: Using fewer vendor sources to achieve greater discounts and higher levels of service.)*	1 2 3 4 5 6 7	1 2 3 4 5 6 7	☐ - ☐ = ☐
Needs/Expectations - Clarifying what major vendors, as well as the store, need/expect from the partnership. *(Examples: Pricing and terms, special promotions, in-person sales calls.)*	1 2 3 4 5 6 7	1 2 3 4 5 6 7	☐ - ☐ = ☐
Systems Integration - Improving the efficiency of product management by teleconnecting with vendors. *(Examples: Sales data exchanges, electronic order processing e.g., automatic reordering.)*	1 2 3 4 5 6 7	1 2 3 4 5 6 7	☐ - ☐ = ☐
Integrated Planning - Collaborating with major vendors to reduce costs and increase sales. *(Example: Codevelopment of written annual plan and calendar to buy, receive, display, market, sell and return each merchandise category.)*	1 2 3 4 5 6 7	1 2 3 4 5 6 7	☐ - ☐ = ☐
Streamline Receiving and Returning - Collaborate with suppliers to streamline receiving and returning. *(Example: Maximize use of publisher bar codes and minimize stickering.)*	1 2 3 4 5 6 7	1 2 3 4 5 6 7	☐ - ☐ = ☐
Market Research - Collaborating with major suppliers to design, implement, and respond to strategic market research. *(Examples: Position the store as an advocate of students; value of "customization" for course materials.)*	1 2 3 4 5 6 7	1 2 3 4 5 6 7	☐ - ☐ = ☐

Store Initiatives
For Vendor Connections:

1. Streamline relationships.

Identify all vendors with whom you presently do business in each major product line. Consider:

- Reducing the number of vendors, where appropriate
- Optimizing (often by reducing) the number of items purchased
- Negotiating improved pricing on fewer items from fewer vendors
- Using buying groups as a vehicle to leverage buying power

2. Develop a vendor plan.

Work with key vendors to identify ways you can collectively reduce the total cost of doing business together, or increase revenues by selling more to the ultimate customer. Cost reduction schemes include:

- Reducing the number of sales calls
- Vendor assisted stock management
- Vendor prepricing of merchandise

Revenue enhancement schemes include:

- On-site support for sales support, stocking, and promotions, where clearly cost justified
- Point of purchase displays
- Improved and integrated stock management system
- Joint customer research (i.e., asking simple questions)

NACS SUPPORT

Services and Projects:

- **Freight program:** NACS has negotiated a number of freight contracts on behalf of college stores (which also can be used by their institutions) which offer substantial discounts on freight shipments. It is estimated that this initiative saves the industry over $10 million per year in freight costs, while generating a small income stream to NACS that has been used to forestall dues increases.

- **Bar code initiative:** NACS has taken the lead in encouraging publishers who are not now bar coding to conform to industry standards. By providing both educational materials and consulting support, NACS hopes to get 50 of the top 100 non-bar coding publishers to begin doing so.

- **Copyright permissions preapproval:** NACS is working with a variety of industry stakeholders to facilitate the development and implementation of technology-based copyright permission preapproval models as noted above.

- **NACSCORP** is responsible for bringing many software manufacturers to the college store market, and for negotiating distribution relationships that allow college stores to provide their customers with substantially lower retail prices on certain software products. Historically, NACSCORP has also facilitated publisher/college store relationships through jointly sponsored promotions.

Professional Development:

- NACS offers several seminars which include sections on working with suppliers, such as Buying of General Merchandise, General Booksellers School, and Textbooks/Course Materials.

NACS SUPPORT

Committees:

- Identifying successful examples of strategic alliances between college stores and non-book vendors, and helping stores understand the priorities of these vendors in selling in our marketplace (the newly appointed Vendor Partnering Task Force)

- Working with publishers on research pertaining to the higher education publishing business (AAP/NACS Higher Education Liaison)

- Assisting in the adoption of non-book Electronic Data Interchange (EDI) in college stores (Retail Systems Advisory)

- Encouraging use of the UPC (Universal Product Code) by college stores and non-book industry vendors (Associate/ Exhibitor Advisory)

- Identifying strategic alliances between college stores and general book publishers (General Book)

- Defining and communicating the key issues for vendors selling into smaller campuses, and the impact on costs (Smaller Stores)

- Defining and communicating issues of hardware, software, and peripheral vendors selling into the campus marketplace (Campus Computer Resellers Alliance)

See the appendix for more details.

CHAPTER 6
COWORKER
CONNECTIONS

A tradition of isolation among coworkers. If the words "we" and "they" are commonly heard in the hallways of your store, you're certainly not alone, but you may be in trouble. This "we/they" mentality effectively partitions organizations of all sizes with walls separating one work group from another, and with ceilings separating "managers" from "workers."

Typically, the larger an organization, the more partitions, and the more deeply embedded "we"/"they" thinking becomes. Examples are easy enough to spot:
- "We" are retailers; "they" are office staff.
- "We" are from books; "they" are from supplies.
- "We" are trade book people; "they" are just textbook people.

See the pattern?

Consider for a moment why this is the case and what its impact is upon our competitive readiness. The answers aren't mysterious. It is that way precisely because we designed it that way, complete with rigid hierarchies, narrowly defined roles, and specialized job descriptions. It's all part and parcel of an antiquated body of management theory extending back to the industrial revolution. The consequences are detrimental to customer service, to employee motivation and teamwork, and to productivity.

Intensifying competition, technological advances, increasing customer expectations, and other changes are challenging us to reinvent the organization itself, to redefine roles and structures, and to reengineer processes so as to connect heretofore isolated people and groups. If our collective success depends upon rapid innovation, it's critical to see that of all the resources at our disposal, "only our people can think" and that "all of us are smarter than any one of us." Is it possible to improve customer service, profitability, average individual compensation, employee participation, and job satisfaction all at the same time? Many today are saying YES!... but no one pretends that it's easy.

Connecting people to purpose. College stores are not buildings, merchandise, or computer systems. We are, more than anything, defined by the people who come together to achieve a common purpose. Only people can define that purpose, determine how best to achieve it, and then implement their decisions. Can anyone doubt that even in this high-tech age, success is ultimately driven more by the human quality of the workplace than by any other single ingredient?

Imagine a business characterized by teamwork, customer service, productivity, and self-management. Such a place does not just spontaneously come about. If it is to exist, it must be preceded by careful and deliberate efforts to develop a consensus about the compelling purpose that brings people together, and to position them so that they are most likely to succeed.

Today's purpose: mission. Long ago, mission statements were dry-as-dust documents created by bureaucracies to facilitate the planning processes of senior management. They were largely irrelevant to employees on the front lines where their success or failure was determined.

It's different today. A well crafted mission statement describes not only what we do and for whom, but also how we do it. When developed properly, it is founded upon deeply held organizational values and is fully aligned with, and supportive of, the broader organizational purpose. It describes today's commitment to deliver outstanding value to customers, to employees, and to owners in terms that are clear and engaging. Good mission statements are written as much for the front line employees as for top management. In fact "if it ain't got zest, it don't pass the test." One who takes "mission" seriously might even be thought of as a "missionary," someone proud to be a part of, and willing to make personal sacrifices for, the store's broader purpose.

Mission indicators. Even if a mission statement captures the very soul of the store, that alone is inadequate. Some old management truisms are worth remembering: "if you can't measure it, you can't manage it," and "what gets measured gets done," because "feedback is the number one motivator." Developing key mission success indicators and providing ongoing feedback are crucial to drive your store forward.

Once you're in a position to measure success, you can more effectively develop the self-management skills of those most closely involved with service delivery. The road to the effective empowerment of staff is paved with training and skill development. Self management presumes the motivation and skill to manage.

Therefore, if you intend to exceed customer expectations, it is first necessary to define what they are, to periodically measure your store's

> *"Imagine a business characterized by teamwork, customer service, productivity, and self-management. Such a place does not just spontaneously come about. If it is to exist, it must be preceded by careful and deliberate efforts to develop a consensus about the compelling purpose that brings people together, and to position them so that they are most likely to succeed."*

performance against them, and to continuously improve those areas identified as weak. Examples of what customers expect and value include reliably stocking the products they need, friendly, responsive, and knowledgeable people to serve them, and fast, efficient, customer friendly operations.

Similarly, if you intend to exceed the reasonable expectations of your employees, you must first define what they are, solicit employee feedback to establish how you rate, and act on areas of deficiency promptly and fairly. Common examples of what employees value include fair compensation, appreciation for outstanding work, involvement in decisions that impact them, and the opportunity to develop professionally.

Developing key mission success indicators and providing ongoing feedback are crucial to drive your store forward.

"Once you're in a position to measure success, you can more effectively develop the management skills of those most closely involved with service delivery"

Lastly, if you intend to exceed the owner's expectations, you must first define them clearly, communicate them to everyone, monitor success in achieving those expectations, and act promptly to continuously improve. Examples include outstanding financial performance (usually exceeding budgeted projections), establishing industry best practice, or leveraging the parent institution's other core goals.

These mission success feedback systems should reach every employee. Understanding and improving on them should become as natural as breathing. That is the real meaning of quality.

Tomorrow's purpose: vision. If mission is defined as the aspirations you have today for your store, vision embodies your dreams for tomorrow. Vision should be values-based, linked to your future customer and your campus, an expression of the yearning to provide legendary value (not just enough to get by), and it must reflect your aspirations for customers, employees, and owners alike.

But dreams without the means to realize them are, after all, just dreams. That's why we need to define "strategic initiatives," specific changes that you will make within two years to move you toward the vision you've embraced. The entire Connections strategy is intended to stimulate thinking about strategic initiatives. Failure to set aside some of today's time to prepare for tomorrow will, most assuredly, leave us unprepared! By contrast, defining these initiatives, scheduling them, and then assigning them both informs and involves everybody, and dramatically increases the likelihood that they will happen. Your vision may be to become a campus hub for the sale of information products, but until you define the strategic initiative to offer expanded services to faculty, and the strategic objective that you personally will contact 50 top faculty in the fall term, your probability of success is zero.

> *"...dreams without the means to realize them are, after all, just dreams. That's why we need to define "strategic initiatives," specific changes that you will make within two years to move you toward the vision you've embraced."*

Individual performance planning. Only after you have defined and measured a service unit's mission, and defined specific strategic initiatives that the unit could accomplish to achieve its vision, are you prepared to do individual performance evaluation and performance planning. Imagine the advantage of knowing where future opportunities are anticipated, and being able to objectively measure success at the time you're considering how best to position and develop the people in your store or department. Yet, I know of no store or business in our industry that has implemented such a complete planning framework. By next year perhaps that will change. Broadly speaking, I believe that this is the biggest untapped business opportunity available to western organizations today!

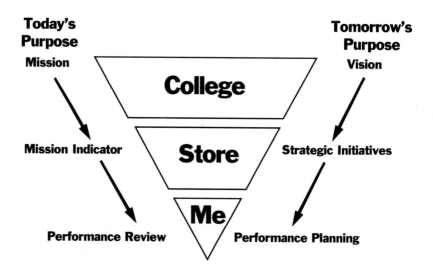

"Imagine the advantage of knowing where future opportunities are anticipated and being able to objectively measure success at the time you're considering how best to position and develop the people in your store or department."

SELF ASSESSMENT

COWORKER CONNECTIONS	A Importance	B Satisfaction	A - B = G Gap
Employee Feedback Systems - Monitoring and responding to coworker perceptions and recommendations. *(Examples: Work climate and leadership surveys, two-way employee/supervisor performance planning.)*	1 2 3 4 5 6 7	1 2 3 4 5 6 7	☐ - ☐ = ☐
Mission Success Indicators - Develop, communicate and train employees in each natural work team in critical success indicators. *(Examples: Customer satisfaction, quality teamwork, financial indicators.)*	1 2 3 4 5 6 7	1 2 3 4 5 6 7	☐ - ☐ = ☐
Core Values - Develop an organization-wide consensus and commitment to core operating values. *(Examples: Truthfulness, respect, stewardship.)*	1 2 3 4 5 6 7	1 2 3 4 5 6 7	☐ - ☐ = ☐
Shared Vision - Develop and communicate a clear, compelling, action-oriented vision statement describing where you intend to be in 3 to 5 years.	1 2 3 4 5 6 7	1 2 3 4 5 6 7	☐ - ☐ = ☐
Strategic Initiatives - Working together to define specific actions and projects 'to do' today that will move your store toward your vision.	1 2 3 4 5 6 7	1 2 3 4 5 6 7	☐ - ☐ = ☐
Matching People to Purpose - Develop a written plan for every employee using mission indicators and the strategic 'to do' list.	1 2 3 4 5 6 7	1 2 3 4 5 6 7	☐ - ☐ = ☐

Store Initiatives
For Coworker Connections

1. Mission.
Develop a mission and mission success indicators for your store.

2. Vision.
Develop a vision and a clearly defined set of strategic initiatives to accomplish it on your campus.

3. Performance planning.
Engage in a performance planning process with all full-time professional staff (including non-management) to define a personal performance plan for each employee:

- How will they contribute to today's mission?

- What is their role in achieving the store's strategic initiatives?

- What core competencies do they need and how will you provide for them? (Include skill development, promotional opportunities, job expansion, etc.)

- Set and stick to staff training goals.

Note: These three steps capture the essence of this book.

4. Organizational structure.
Reconsider your organizational structure. Does it reflect the way your organization actually runs? Should run?

- Does it maximize customer service?

- Does it allow the flexibility required by the new work ethic and family issues?

Store Initiatives
For Coworker Connections

- Read *Zapp! The Lightning of Empowerment* by William Byham. An excellent book and quick read, it outlines a process for empowering people.

- Create a succession plan for key positions in your store.

5. Management style.
Re-examine your management style:

- Are staff members full participants in decisions that affect their jobs?

- Are you rewarding excellent customer service?

- Does each person know his/her importance to the store's mission/vision?

- Are you aware of people's personal goals, and do you support them?

- Learn about 360-degree reviews, and see if they are already in place (or supported) by any area on campus.

NACS SUPPORT

Professional Development:

- The NACS Merchandising Center has a variety of human resource and management issues videos.

- NACS offers the Managing With People seminar.

Committees :

- Helping stores develop 360-degree performance feedback systems, encouraging stores to include employees at all levels in development of mission and vision, and developing a succession model for planning store management succession (The newly appointed Human Potential Committee)

- Identifying successful models where "diverse" thinking has been incorporated into decision-making processes in college stores (Cultural Diversity)

- Developing methodology to enable college store management to understand the importance of developing and implementing succession management strategies (Professional development)

See the appendix for more details.

CHAPTER 7
CLOSING REFLECTIONS
ABOUT CONNECTIONS

Change isn't what it used to be. It doesn't take an economist to predict that the next few years will bring increasing fiscal pressures, rapidly rising customer expectations, and intensified competition. At the same time, unprecedented shifts are underway both in the definition of "course materials" and the methods by which they can be distributed and paid for.

These times call for a fundamental rethinking of what we do, and how core stakeholders can work together to do it better. To accomplish this, we must overcome deeply embedded traditions of isolation. Connecting in new and creative ways to customers, to campus colleagues, to key vendor representatives, and to our own coworkers may well be the single most powerful key to competitive advantage in the '90s.

These connections can only occur when someone on campus takes the leadership to constructively structure new relationships. That someone must be you! To be successful, we must know our purpose and how well we're accomplishing it. Our mission must be clear and success must be measurable. We also need to know where we're going, and allocate at least part of today's resources to prepare for it. That means more than an engaging vision about your role on campus; you must also have a strategy for getting there. That's why it is imperative to have defined a dozen or so strategic initiatives. These initiatives are specific projects or tasks that can be accomplished in one to two years, and that will move you in the direction you've consciously planned.

We are not about to experience a revolution, as some overly zealous futurists predict. However, "business as usual" is no longer an available option. At the end of this decade, the traditional textbook market will still be substantial, many stores will still operate in relative isolation from their campus community, most corporate links will still be based purely on short-range utilitarian goals, and there will be no shortage of autocrats in our businesses to prescribe in detail exactly who must do what and when. They will just be fewer in number! The odds are dramatically shifted in our favor if we have spent these intervening years defining and implementing strategic initiatives that connect us to our customers, our campus, our key vendor representatives, and our coworkers in ways that foster mutual advantage. That's the message I've tried to convey here, and the purpose of my brief leadership as the president of NACS.

> **"We are not about to experience a revolution as some overly zealous futurists predict. However, 'business as usual' is no longer an available option..."**
>
> **"The odds are dramatically shifted in our favor if we have spent these intervening years defining and implementing strategic initiatives that connect us to our customers, our campus, our key vendor representatives, and our coworkers in ways that foster mutual advantage. That's the message I've tried to convey here and the purpose of my brief leadership as the president of NACS."**

EPILOGUE
THE COMMUNITY CONNECTION

The community connection. The core thesis of "Connections" is that our organizations are people (coworkers) serving people (customers), usually in partnership with others on and off campus who have a stake in our success. However, we also have a certain duty, as good stewards of the community we live in, that goes beyond narrowly defined business interests. It is the duty to manage the environment in such a fashion that it is an inheritance to our grandchildren, and to treat all people with the same respect and dignity that we cherish from others, even when they look, behave, and think somewhat differently. It is this duty of citizenship that connects us to conscience in such a fashion that we behave rightly, even when there is no immediate reward.

Synergy: the common core of connections. Synergy is the concept that, under the right circumstances, "one plus one" can equal more than "two". It occurs when stakeholders who have different skills and assets consciously work together to create a bigger pie, rather than confront each other over how to split up a fixed one. **Wherever there are common interests and interdependencies, there is opportunity for synergy — a principle worth considering as you select your store's strategic initiatives and partners.**

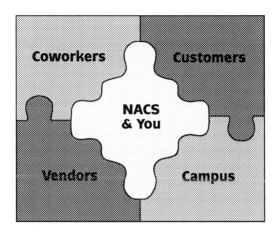

Appendix I: NACS Strategic Focus Summary

This document summarizes the results, as of July 1993, of a comprehensive, professionally-facilitated, long-range planning process by the National Association of College Stores. The process involved an amazing amount of time and energy from more industry leaders than can be listed here, and included members of the NACS Board of Trustees as well as representatives from the NACSCORP and CSREF Boards, and other industry groups.

The goal was to analyze the trends facing the industry in the next decade, and realign as many of NACS' resources and activities as possible to focus on helping our members to compete, now and in the future.

Through a variety of industry task forces, committee and staff work, and at the direction of the NACS Board of Trustees, significant progress has been made, and continues to be made, on the four "strategic initiatives" described within this document. Those results have been, and will continue to be, communicated to the membership through articles, educational sessions and other activities.

Succeeding In A Rapidly Changing World:
A New Strategic Focus For The Association
The Results of the NACS Board's Long-Range Planning Meetings

All of us in the college store industry are on the verge of experiencing the most pervasive changes in our history. Over the past year the NACS Board has engaged in a series of strategic planning sessions to examine the most significant of the shifts in our business and to plan a series of initiatives to address them.

We identified the three most important trends as:

1. **The transition taking place in the traditional textbook.** In the wake of the information revolution, the industry's core product is moving from a market dominated by new and used textbooks to one which includes coursepacks, customized books, and a growing variety of products evolving from digital text, sound, video, and graphics.

2. **Intensifying competition.**
   On campus: With the growing variety of information products, college stores will face increasingly intense competition: from campus libraries with their strong faculty connection and expanding entrepreneurial activities; academic computing centers with their technology base and expertise; copy shops (on and off campus) with their capability to produce and sell coursepacks; publishers who are experimenting with new technologies delivered in new ways, and others.

   Off campus: Competition is also intensifying for our other major products. Our customers are sophisticated shoppers, looking for the combination of quality, service, and value (price) offered by off-campus contenders such as Walmart, K-Mart, warehouse clubs, specialty catalog retailers, and category superstores.

3. **Using technology to run our stores more efficiently.** Stores will use technology to gain competitive advantage to reduce costs and enhance services. This will go beyond text and point-of-sales systems as the industry's most progressive stores use networks to build links to vendors, to financial institutions and to their local campus.

The implications of these trends:

Embedded in these trends is an unprecedented opportunity to integrate the campus store into the fabric of college life and have far-reaching implications for the industry we serve, and in turn, the services it will require. On one thing we are very clear: The winners in the next decade will deliver outstanding value to all of their major stakeholders:

- Customers, by delivering legendary service,
- Employees, by developing high-performance self-managing teams, and
- Owners, by delivering exceptional financial performance and effectively supporting the campus mission.

It is the Board's belief that our industry's future may well depend upon the preparations undertaken in the next few years...preparations designed to improve our stores' abilities to compete and to increase the efficiency of our operations and the quality of our service.

To that end, the Board will encourage our committees and task forces, our professional development, our market research, our publications, and the annual meeting program to focus on these three issues.

Four strategic initiatives will be undertaken this year:

In addition, it was the Board's decision to establish several major new initiatives focused on these issues. Next year, when the initial projects are well underway, it is our intent to add additional initiatives to our project list.

1. **We will facilitate the development of a copyright preagreement system.**

The first step in the transition of the textbook has been a move by faculty toward custom publishing. Faculty and students believe customized materials deliver relevant information in a highly convenient (and more cost-effective) format.

Yet many college stores are not serving their campus's demand for this product, and many publishers have not recognized the potential income opportunity created by allowing the reproduction of articles and chapters in coursepacks. In both cases, the ease of copyright administration and acquisition is a major factor in fulfilling demand for these materials.

We will be working with publishers, the Copyright Clearance Center, and other stakeholders to develop a systematic, coordinated process of securing copyright permissions. Our intention is to facilitate the development of a preagreement process in which stores request, report, and pay for materials in a single (electronic) step which also satisfies publishers' needs for accurate, complete and auditable data.

Our goal is to have a pilot copyright preagreement project underway by April, 1994.

In addition, we will campaign to communicate the custom publishing opportunity to both stores and publishers; we will develop programs to educate college stores about this business.

2. We will become an active participant in the American Association For Higher Education's "Textbook Of The Future" project and will consider another major faculty research initiative.

We believe competing successfully in the new world means changing the interaction between college stores and one of our core constituencies, the faculty.

We believe college stores need to position ourselves on campus away from serving faculty as textbook purchasing and sales agents ("book butlers") to a consultative relationship in which we assist faculty in the selection of the most appropriate information products for students ("curriculum consultants").

The Board has enthusiastically endorsed and will consider helping to fund a proposal from the American Association For Higher Education (AAHE) to study the future of the textbook to "understand, facilitate, and guide major changes in the tools and materials of instruction."

We believe our participation in the AAHE project will improve our understanding of the new information products and publicly position college stores as agents of change on campus.

We will be considering another major research initiative into the way faculty choose and use their course materials; we will create professional development and communication programs for college stores designed to improve interaction with faculty.

3. We will support NACSCORP's efforts to help college stores compete.

Sales of other primary products, especially school supplies, are being lost to competitors, and others are being replaced by technology.

Increased sales of custom-published materials, combined with lower prices for such materials and a potential decline in the used book market, may lead to declining gross sales and profit dollars for the industry.

The Board recognizes that the industry must look for new products to supplement lost revenues. We strongly support NACSCORP's initiatives to develop, and to support with merchandising tools, a market for college stores in computer software, computer peripherals and media, and other leading-edge products.

We will support NACSCORP's efforts to provide medium and small stores with methods to be competitive in these areas, and we support NACSCORP's investigation of new product categories to help all stores be more competitive.

4. We have begun a major bar code initiative to encourage publishers and manufacturers to place standardized bar codes on all units shipped to college stores.

To improve efficiency and increase customer service, many college stores are purchasing and implementing point-of-sale (POS) systems. To better realize the benefits of POS, the Board believes NACS has an important role in facilitating standardization in the market.

Specifically, the effective use of point-of-sale systems requires consistent application by publishers and manufacturers of bar codes according to EAN and UPC standards that already exist in the market. Eliminating the need to apply labels to most units sold by college stores (and to have to remove them for returns) will save the industry millions of dollars in labor, paperwork, and human error.

By April, 1994, we will have identified the one hundred largest publishers and other industry suppliers who are not currently bar coding their products consistently.

Simultaneously, with the support of a number of industry partners, we will develop an initiative to educate, encourage, and support the application of bar codes by all publishers and manufacturers not currently complying with bar code standards.

Our goal is to have 50 of the top 100 firms agree to begin bar coding no later than Summer, 1994.

Three additional components:

The Board believes that to achieve maximum success, three additional components must be integral to our work:

1. Including all industry stakeholders.

We believe that the success of NACS' efforts to secure the future of the industry requires the active participation of all stakeholders, including institutional, private, and contract-managed stores; associate members, related associations, and others.

We have included a variety of groups in the development of this plan and shall expand and improve our efforts to ensure that all major stakeholders are involved in the initiatives that evolve from it.

For one major stakeholder group, the staff, these initiatives will provide new direction to their work, will require acquisition of new competencies, and may lead to some restructuring.

The result should be a more focused and inclusive association, with the Board moving, as one member suggested, "from managing an association to leading an industry."

2. A well-thought-out financing plan.

To ensure their success, each of these initiatives will require a substantial investment by NACS, although the exact amounts are not yet determined. As part of our planning process, the Board considered a variety of financing methods. These methods include abandoning some services no longer serving a significant number of members' needs, postponing the hiring of a field staff person and reallocating already-approved budget funds to the implementation of this strategy, raising dues or raising the prices of some products or services, working with CSREF to secure funding; and soliciting funds from outside sources.

We have asked the Board's Budget and Finance Committee to submit a funding proposal to the Board in December. Until we approve a comprehensive funding plan, we decided to delay hiring a field staff person and have allocated those funds for this fiscal year to begin implementing the initiatives.

3. **Integrating a comprehensive communications program into the process.**

Initially, any major shift in direction of an organization may cause confusion. It is the Board's intent to construct a communications plan to members, committees, staff, and other interested organizations that defines these strategies and actions in a way that reinforces the need to focus the organization's energy on them and to commit the organization's limited resources to them.

This document is intended as a preliminary step in the communications process. Your comments, questions and concerns are most welcome, and should be addressed to any member of the Board, to Garis Distelhorst, executive director of NACS, or to any of the senior managers of the association.

"The winners in the next decade will deliver outstanding value to all of their major stakeholders..."

(customers, campus, corporate partners, and coworkers.)

"To that end, the Board will encourage our committees and task forces, our professional development, our market research, our publications, and the annual meeting program to focus on...preparations designed to improve our stores' ability to compete..."

NACS Board of Trustees

Appendix II: NACS Committees & Task Forces

The NACS Leadership used the "Connections" framework as a major component in setting NACS committee objectives for 1994/95. The goal was to identify a number of significant things NACS could accomplish through committee work which would facilitate our members' efforts to develop and accomplish their own "to do" lists of strategic projects.

The work of the volunteers who serve on committees and task forces is crucial to accomplishing the goals of the Association, and to communicate the Connections message and provide assistance to members. The 1994/95 committees were asked to undertake "strategic objectives" that support the Connections framework in addition to, and in support of, work on their "operational objectives," which typically consist of developing articles, annual meeting sessions, surveys, and other activities.

Listed below are the "strategic objectives" for each committee. For further information about the committee activities, please consult the 1994/95 Committee Handbook (available from NACS) or contact NACS for the name of the Committee Chair.

AAP/NACS Higher Education Liaison

STRATEGIC OBJECTIVES:
To Facilitate Vendor and Campus Connections...

    A. Contribute to and/or cosponsor research pertaining to the higher education publishing business such as faculty selection and use of course materials and trends and volume in the coursepack business.

To Facilitate Vendor Connections...

    B. Find the cooperative points in the organizations' two strategic plans to identify areas for collaboration, especially with respect to copyright clearance, compliance, and textbook price perceptions.

To Facilitate Vendor Connections...

    C. Working with the Vendor Partnering Task Force, define and communicate to the industry the key issues for textbook publishers in relation to selling into the campus marketplace. Examples might include:
- The cost of providing ancillary materials in the face of declining unit sales
- The need to provide customized materials/packages to satisfy faculty desires
- Problems in communicating and shipping updated versions of books and/or packaging books with supplements

Annual Meeting Committee

STRATEGIC OBJECTIVES:
To Facilitate All Connections...

    A. Coordinate and facilitate delivery of educational sessions at the St. Louis Annual Meeting on the strategic initiatives accomplished by NACS and each committee.

To Facilitate All Connections...
>   B. Develop a theme and logo for the 1995 Annual Meeting that incorporates the concept of "connections."

To Facilitate All Connections...
>   C. Continue to integrate the Professional Development Committee into the planning of the Annual Meeting program (including general session speakers, etc.).

To Facilitate Customer Connections...
>   D. Help the industry understand the impact of changing course materials on the market, consider creating a 1 or 1-1/2 day "bonus" breakthrough session at the 1995 Annual Meeting Session on the future of course materials.

Associate/Exhibitor Advisory Committee

STRATEGIC OBJECTIVES:
To Facilitate Vendor Connections...
>   A. Work with other NACS committees (e.g. Retail Systems Advisory and Vendor Partnering Task Force) to encourage incorporation of UPC into non-book item pricing.

To Facilitate Vendor Connections...
>   B. Advise the NACS Professional Development Committee and Ongoing CSREF Board as to how associate members can be increasingly included in education, research initiatives, and NACS committee work.

Campus Computer Resellers Alliance

STRATEGIC OBJECTIVES:
(NOTE: While NACS has never asked CCRA to accomplish specific objectives, in the concept of partnering we propose the following objectives that CCRA might consider to support the strategic initiatives of NACS and NACS committees.)

To Facilitate Vendor Connections...
>   A. Define and communicate to college stores the key issues of hardware, software, and peripheral vendors selling into the campus marketplace, being specific by product line where appropriate. (Include site licensing issues in this communication.)

To Facilitate Campus Connections...
>   B. Where computer resale doesn't take place through the college store, identify and describe successful strategic alliances between college stores and campus resellers.

To Facilitate Campus Connections...

   C. Identify and describe successful strategic alliances between college stores/ campus microcenters and other groups on campus, such as academic computing or media centers.

To Facilitate Vendor Connections...

   D. Identify and describe successful alliances between college stores/campus microcenters and hardware and/or software vendors, including:

- Campus site licensing agreements administered by college stores or campus microcenters
- Where vendors have paid for on-site assistance for stores/microcenters during selling seasons

Certification Committee

STRATEGIC OBJECTIVES:
To Facilitate All Connections...

   A. Develop methodology for measuring industry best practices /benchmarking and add them to the point system for the program.

   B. Identify the core competencies required by college stores to serve their campus in the 1990s. For example:

1. Having a vision and a plan which fully integrate the store into the campus
2. Researching and incorporating the customer's needs and expectations into the plan
3. Seeking out and incorporating the expectation of the owner(s) into the plan
4. Empowering store personnel to deliver quality service to customers
5. Thoroughly understanding the store's financial performance
6. Implementing technology where it can enhance customer service and/or improve efficiency and financial performance
7. Actively collaborating with "partners" on and off campus
8. A fundamental understanding of the college store business at an operations/retail management level

College Store Evaluation Committee

STRATEGIC OBJECTIVES:
To Facilitate All Connections...

   A. Add characteristics to the evaluation process that will evaluate the efforts of college stores to connect to customers, their campus, vendor partners, and coworkers.

To Facilitate All Connections...

    B. Integrate into the CSES Program work by other NACS Committees to identify and develop industry benchmarks and best practices.

To Facilitate All Connections...

    C. Working with the Successful Practices and Benchmarks Task Force, identify operational benchmarks for the industry which might include such items as:

- Student waiting time in line at "rush"
- Inventory turnover in key product areas
- Percent of textbooks in-stock on the first day of classes
- Customer relations benchmarks

Community/Junior/Technical College Stores Committee

STRATEGIC OBJECTIVES:

To Facilitate Customer Connections...

    A. Identify and communicate to college stores and industry vendors national student demographic trends. Relate how the changing student population could impact specific customer groups' service requirements and product needs such as the requirements and needs of:

- Distance learners
- Life-long learners
- An older traditional student
- A more sophisticated 18-22 year-old

To Facilitate Customer Connections...

    B. Identify for the industry the specific issues faced by community/junior/ technical college stores in serving their customers.

Cultural Diversity Committee

STRATEGIC OBJECTIVES:

To Facilitate All Connections...

    A. Identify successful models where "diverse" thinking has been actively incorporated into decision-making processes in college stores to improve the quality of the decisions.

To Facilitate Customer Connections...

    B. Identify product and service issues that stores and vendors should know relative to serving specific cultural and ethnic groups on campus.

To Facilitate Coworker Connections...
   C. Identify other industries' efforts that have been successful in creating a more diverse constituency, and review for possible application those efforts that could be successful in the college store community.

Environmental Concerns Committee

STRATEGIC OBJECTIVES:
To Facilitate Customer Connections...
   A. Develop a model to help stores promote their own environmental programs in order to be acknowledged on campus as leading/participating in campus-wide environment efforts.

To Facilitate Campus Connections...
   B. Develop methodology which enables college stores to partner with other campus entities and/or local community to promote sale and use of environmentally sound products.

To Facilitate All Connections...
   C. Assist stores in gaining feedback and communicating ways in which the sale and use of ecologically aware products contribute to the stores' relationships with customers, campus, vendors, and employees.

Financial Survey Committee

STRATEGIC OBJECTIVES:
To Facilitate Campus Connections...
   A. Create or identify model communications/documents to present financial performance information to the campus including the administration, students, and faculty.

To Facilitate Campus Connections...
   B. Identify industry financial "best practices" and financial benchmarks for college stores, basing it on (and providing input to) the NACUBO benchmark project. (Address the variety of different benchmarks that are required depending on campus demographics, size, type of school, store size, etc.)

To Facilitate Campus Connections...
   C. Develop the capability for stores to develop customized comparisons of financial data.

General Book Committee

STRATEGIC OBJECTIVES:

To Facilitate Vendor Connections...

A. Define and communicate to college stores the key issues for general book publishers selling into the campus marketplace. Examples might include:
- The cost of having sales representatives call on smaller, geographically diverse stores.
- The high percentage of sales through distributors, which interferes with a direct understanding of the market.

To Facilitate Vendor Connections...

B. Identify successful examples of strategic alliances between college stores and general book publishers, including:
- Special in-store promotions for author visits.
- Successful agency plan agreements.

To Facilitate Vendor Connections...

C. Work with the LSG Bookseller Advisory Group on their proposed initiatives with publishers in order to benefit all stores.

Health Science Stores Committee

STRATEGIC OBJECTIVES:

To Facilitate All Connections...

A. Define financial and operational benchmarks unique to this group.

To Facilitate Customer Connections...

B. With health science being a leading area in use of new "course materials" identify for the industry things all college stores can learn from the direction being taken by new health science teaching tools, specifically on CD-ROM.

Human Potential Committee

STRATEGIC OBJECTIVES:

To Facilitate Coworker Connections...

A. Develop a system that stores can use to gain 360-degree performance feedback (feedback from staff at all levels-senior, peer, and subordinate). Integrate this information on a national basis to create benchmarks and to measure work climate quality and leadership.

To Facilitate Coworker Connections...
  B. Develop a program to encourage stores to include store employees at all
  levels in development of the store's mission/vision, and identify successful
  cases where "inclusive" participation has been actively incorporated into the
  decision-making process.

To Facilitate Coworker Connections...
  C. Develop a model for succession planning that can be customized and used
  by stores of all sizes and types.

To Facilitate Coworker Connections...
  D. Develop or locate model training and professional development programs
  for store staff that can be customized by individual members (include
  development of model programs to assist staff in identifying personal goals
  for an individual's development).

Institutional Stores/Campus Relations Committee

STRATEGIC OBJECTIVES:
To Facilitate Campus Connections...
  A. Identify successful ways being used by college stores to get consensus with
  campus administration on a store's mission, vision and performance
  standards. Working with the Professional Development Committee, assist
  stores in defining a mission/vision that supports the institution's mission/vision.

To Facilitate Campus Connections...
  B. Take steps to understand and communicate to the industry the needs and
  interests of key potential partners on campus (including campus computing,
  academic computing, libraries, print shop, administrators, registrar, media
  center...). Then, for this group of campus partners:
  • Identify common issues
  • Identify industry "good practices" where collaboration has already
    been established
  • Develop a model plan stores can use to facilitate collaboration

To Facilitate Campus Connections...
  C. Define ways stores can use campus networks to better serve campus constituencies.

LSG Steering Committee

STRATEGIC OBJECTIVES:

To Facilitate All Connections...

Encourage collaboration among members of the Large Stores Group in endeavors to enhance campus relations, utilize technology to run stores more effectively and partner to help all college stores become more competitive.

Merchandising Committee

STRATEGIC OBJECTIVES:

To Facilitate Customer Connections...

   A. Identify industry benchmarks for maximizing use of space:
   - Clarify how this use varies depending on available facilities and campus served.
   - Identify successful development and use of flex-space.
   - Provide a list of resources for the flooring, fixturing and other items required to implement this activity.

To Facilitate Customer Connections...

   B. Identify stores that have successfully used remote locations, kiosks, and carts to serve customers and communicate sales/margin/personnel issues and benchmarks.

Nominating—Associate Trustee (Supplier) Nominating Committee

STRATEGIC OBJECTIVES:

To Facilitate Vendor Connections...

   A. Recommend to the chair of the Nominating Committee a candidate for Associate Supplier Trustee to serve a two-year term on the NACS Board of Trustees beginning in April.

To Facilitate Vendor Connections...

   B. Review the criteria for the selection of Associate Supplier Trustee and make recommendations to the NACS Board if changes are deemed necessary.

To Facilitate All Connections...

   C. Submit to the membership a full slate of well-qualified and capable persons to serve NACS as officers and trustees having considered all such members as potential candidates and taking into account the demographic make-up of the NACS membership.

To Facilitate All Connections...
   D. Recommend to future Nominating Committees improvements in the
      nominating process.

Privately Owned Stores Committee

STRATEGIC OBJECTIVES:
To Facilitate All Connections...
   Identify and recommend for the industry ways to enhance communication
   between on- and off-campus college stores.

Professional Development Committee

STRATEGIC OBJECTIVES:
   A. Coordinate educational and professional development opportunities within
      NACS focusing on the strategic initiatives by:
      • acting as a liaison with the Program Committee in developing
        educational offerings at the Annual Meeting which complement the
        NACS strategic initiatives.
      • partnering with the Meetings & Expositions Department, along with
        CSREF, CCRA, and other NACS, Inc. departments and entities, to
        develop forums, special topic sessions, and/or publications which address
        the NACS strategic initiatives.
      • exploring the particular educational opportunities which result from the
        work of the Successful Practices & Benchmarks Task Force.
      • coordinating with allied associations or industry groups a minimum of
        two programs which emphasize the NACS strategic initiatives.
      • collaborating with state and regional associations to develop educational
        programs of mutual interest which support the NACS strategic initiatives.

   B. Develop tools and programs (which may include one to three hour or one
      day workshops) which strengthen the NACS strategic initiatives by utilizing
      current materials or creating new materials to:

      Connect to the Campus
      - teach college stores how to use the *College Store Planning: A Mission &
        Vision Kit* as a tool for their own store (possible task force).

      - utilize the resources developed by the Institutional Store/Campus
        Relations Committee as a means for strengthening the college store's
        relationship with its campus and identifying best practices in this area for
        college store (possible task force).

- teach college store managers how to work better with their bosses and other business-related personnel, including how to gain consensus (possible task force).

Connect to Co-workers
- enable college store management to understand the importance of developing and implementing succession management strategies to ensure professional transition when management changes (possible task force, utilize the results of the CHEMA study, link with Human Potential Committee).

Connect to Customers
- encourage college stores to use the *College Stores Service Quality Research Kit* as an instrument for strengthening the store's relationship to its customer base (possible task force).

- train stores to reverse the "high price image" of the college store on campus (possible task force, link with Textbook Perceptions Task Force).

Connect to Vendors
- explore the particular educational opportunities that result from the work of the Vendor Partnering Task Force.

C. Work with staff and committee members with systems expertise to help strengthen members' knowledge, and use of technology as a method for increasing the competitive opportunities for college stores, to include but not be limited to:

   • developing an electronic bulletin board format to use as a followup to educational programs.
   • developing follow-up training using e-mail as a communication tool.
   • explore educational opportunities arising from the work of the Retail Systems Advisory and other committees' technological resources.

Publications Advisory Committee

STRATEGIC OBJECTIVES:
To Facilitate All Connections...
   A. Share articles from other retail and higher education periodicals with the editorial staff that would be appropriate for reprinting in NACS publications.

To Facilitate All Connections...
    B. Identify ways NACS can present publications in electronic forms.

To Facilitate All Connections...
    C. Proactively report on the "connections" issues and success stories (and technology needs) on campus.

Retail Systems Advisory Committee

STRATEGIC OBJECTIVES:
To Facilitate Vendor Connections...
    A. Assist in the development of and monitor changes to general retail industry and college store industry standards for Electronic Data Interchange (EDI) and machine-readable coding (Bar Codes) for merchandise and product cartons.

To Facilitate Vendor Connections...
    B. Maintain a product knowledge base on retail technology systems and trends as well as a personnel resource pool from the college store industry.

To Facilitate Vendor Connections...
    C. Identify manageable and obtainable strategic initiatives for college stores of all sizes, assist with the implementation of new retail technology, increase utilization of existing technology (i.e. PUBNET), and/or to integrate existing systems (i.e. text, trade, etc.) with other system modules.

To Facilitate All Connections...
    D. Assist with the connectivity of college stores to on-line databases, services, campus networks, and the Internet.

Smaller Stores Committee

STRATEGIC OBJECTIVES:
To Facilitate All Connections...
    A. Identify ways small stores can overcome size to achieve efficiency of scale in operations, training, and especially in utilizing technology as a means of gaining a competitive edge in the college store market. (Working with the Retail Systems Advisory Committee.)

To Facilitate Vendor Connections...
    B. Define and communicate to college stores the key issues for vendors selling into smaller campuses, and how these impact on smaller stores' costs. Examples might include:

- The cost of travel versus average order size
- The percentage of a particular vendor's line that might be stocked by a smaller store.

To Facilitate All Connections...

    C. Implement initiatives which result in larger numbers of small stores regularly using E-mail on campus and to communicate among themselves.

Successful Practices & Benchmarks Task Force

STRATEGIC OBJECTIVES:
To Facilitate All Connections...

    A. Identify successful practices in the industry, using sources such as the NACUBO Awards Program and the LSG Idea Exchange, and communicate these practices to members. Practices should be organized around building connections to customers, campus partners, coworkers and vendors.

To Facilitate All Connections...

    B. Identify benchmarks in the industry (use NACUBO Benchmarking Program as a starting point, but provide feedback for improvements) building on connections to:

- customers —customer service focus (e.g. waiting time in line, perception surveys, o/s by product line);
- campus partners — financial and service focus (e.g. TO, GMROI, Sales/ Ft., Sales/Employee);
- coworkers — employee satisfaction focus (e.g. standard employee climate survey);
- vendors — vendor relations focus (e.g. jointly save money, explore new markets, take advantage of opportunities).

To Facilitate All Connections...

    C. Link the identification and monitoring of benchmarks to the charges of other committees, such as College Store Evaluation (see objective F.), Financial Survey (See objective E.) and Certification.

To Facilitate All Connections...

    D. Build a flexible, selective model for benchmark comparisons (e.g. Financial Survey results — allow for individualized selection of "peer" group).

To Facilitate All Connections...

    E. Working with the College Store Evaluation Committee, develop criteria for reviewing examples of successful practices and benchmarks, giving special consideration to practices that build connections to customers, campus partners, coworkers and vendors.

To Facilitate All Connections...

F. Develop an awards process that recognizes industry examples of successful practices in connections that college stores develop with customers, employees, vendor partners and/or the campus.

Textbook/Course Materials Committee

STRATEGIC OBJECTIVES:

To Facilitate Customer Connections...

A. Work with the USC Center for Scholarly Technology to develop a tool to assess the readiness of a given campus for new products.

To Facilitate Campus Connections...

B. Take steps to determine what faculty value or want from the college store and develop a strategy to respond to it. (Work with other initiatives such as the AAHE Teaching Materials of the Future study.)

To Facilitate Campus Connections...

C. Improve college store/faculty relationships, identify successful examples, or develop an outline for a program(s) stores could offer to orient faculty about:
- Textbook adoptions
- Custom publishing and copyright
- New technology

To Facilitate Customer and Campus Connections...

D. Create the following educational materials (pamphlets):
- How to start up a custom publishing business, including how to develop a custom publishing mission statement
- How to obtain copyright permission
- A booklet that stores could give to parents of incoming freshman students
- A briefing kit for editors of school newspapers to use on questions about textbook prices (Working with the Textbook Price Perception Task Force).

To Facilitate Campus Connections...

E. Facilitate connections between libraries and college stores by creating a "white" paper from information gathered from current reserve room projects (i.e. San Diego State, Penn State, UConn).

Textbook Perceptions Task Force

STRATEGIC OBJECTIVES:
To Facilitate Customer Connections...

    A. Develop a hands-on communications/public relations program for college stores that deals with the problems of textbook price perceptions by students, using one "typical" campus as a "laboratory" to create a model that can be used by the entire industry.

To Facilitate Customer Connections...

    B. Identify successful examples of existing store programs that have improved the store's communication with customers, and share them with the industry in a workable format for all store types.

To Facilitate Customer Connections...

    C. Determine how to assist stores in using existing tools.

Vendor Partnering Task Force

STRATEGIC OBJECTIVES:
To Facilitate Vendor Connections...

    A. Identify where successful alliances between college stores and their non-book vendors have occurred and develop methodology for sharing this information with all segments of the membership.

- Where vendors have provided stores with on-site assistance during selling seasons.
- Ways in which vendor inventory information has been made available to store's customers.
- Direct selling on campus by sales reps in support of store objectives.
- Ways stores have helped vendors understand their needs and have seen vendors change policies or procedures to reflect this new understanding.

To Facilitate Vendor Connections...

    B. Develop tools to assist stores in understanding vendor needs.

- Should be the development of an open, flexible survey which can measure specific vendor requirements for production and sales.

To Facilitate Vendor Connections...

    C. Review products and tools currently available through NACS and recommend how they can be used to develop stronger partnerships between stores and their vendors.

- Bar Code Initiative
- PUBNET
- New NACS Director of Retail Systems Information
- NACSCORP

ABOUT THE AUTHOR

Richard W. McDaniel, CSP
Director of Business Services
Cornell University, Ithaca, NY

Having served the industry on scores of committees, task forces, and educational programs, Rich was elected the president of the National Association of College Stores for 1994/95. Words commonly used to describe him include 'futurist,' 'innovator' and 'leader.' Upon completing graduate studies in business administration at Cornell he joined the staff of the Campus Store, where he has enthusiastically invested most of the last two decades. During that period the store's staff have pioneered in the cost-effective application of technologies extending from early automation of all internal business functions to current cutting-edge research and development work in electronic custom publishing and networked desktop services. Other innovations include an award-winning space management system, development of a consolidated campus-wide ID card system and the design and construction of a collegiate shopping mall.

Yet in recent years it has been human innovations, even more than technical or design, that have become the center of attention at Cornell. Rich serves there as a member of the University Quality Council, a TQM leadership body, and is actively seeking to implement more participative, humane, and productive approaches to doing business together.

Rich and his wife, Gretchen, live in Covert, New York with their three children. Leisure hours find Rich restoring their historic Greek Revival home or jogging along the dirt roads of Covert.

"Our management team has developed basic initiatives for our store such as mission and vision, but we have not gone as in-depth as the Connections strategy, which will provide a foundation to help us further develop strategic initiatives such as more partnering on campus, becoming more pro-active so we are better prepared for the future. The Connections framework gives NACS volunteers and committee members a solid foundation to identify and implement strategic initiatives to accomplish their objectives. As each NACS committee focuses on its objectives and considers the Connections model to determine what will be in the best interest of the NACS membership, I think this will be an invaluable tool and will help us to bring the membership closer together."

—Peggy Falgien, CSP, Manager, University Bookstore, University of Wyoming, Laramie, WY

"Rich's book has helped me immeasurably in illuminating all the traffic signs along the 'Data-way,' signs which virtually serve as connecting links between NACS, the bookstore, co-workers and customers. Rich's book is perfectly timed in light of all the changes we face in the industry."

—Kathy Anderson, General Book Buyer, UCSD Bookstore, University of California/San Diego, La Jolla, CA

"The lists of sample store initiatives at the end of each chapter are invaluable...many are actions for our annual business plan. They all stimulate thinking of ways to weave the store into the fabric of intellectual and campus life at Vanderbilt. Thanks for a very useful book!"

—John Turk, CSP, Director of Bookstores, Vanderbilt University, Nashville, TN

"In the epic novel *Gone With the Wind* the heroine, Scarlett O'Hara, often postponed decisions awaiting a better 'tomorrow.' Well, 'tomorrow' is here in the college market. It's time to be decisive about changing the very essence of how we do business. The old strategies don't work anymore. We now have to redefine relationships with our campus, our customers, our employees and our vendors in order to remain competitive. *Connections* is an action-plan to help stores define 'today' so that there will be a 'tomorrow.'"

—Tommye Miller, CSP, Director, Valdosta State University Bookstore, Valdosta, GA

"Rich is pulling, pushing, and prodding us along the path to our future and the future of college stores. Some of us go more enthusiastically than others, but he points a clear and necessary path."

—Gerald E. Colver, CSP, Director, Lafayette College Store, Easton, PA

"We have been talking and worrying about the changes facing the college store industry. Wake-up calls, focused mission statements, articulated visions, and strategic planning are some of the ways in which we have tried to deal with these changes. Not everyone likes change. Some of us are afraid of change and some of us hate change! *Connections* puts all of the fear and worry into perspective by pulling together the key issues with several practical and specific suggestions that any one of us can implement. But most importantly, Rich McDaniel reminds us that people are the key to the implementation of change. If we value the people inside and outside the bookstore, we can begin to make the right connections."

—Carol Marrin, CSP, Director, St. John's University Bookstore, Collegeville, MN; and College of St. Benedict Bookstore, St. Joseph, MN

"*Connections* provides a wonderful framework for booksellers to work in partnership with their customers and their suppliers. I think the store that embraces the *Connections* philosophy will have a wonderful reputation on campus."

—Michael Melody, Executive Vice President, College & Software Publishing, Houghton-Mifflin Company, Boston, MA

"*Connections* should be required reading for any higher education professional involved in college stores in any way: bookstore managers, buyers, department heads, as well as auxiliary services directors and business managers. It's a concise, well-written handbook which discusses the bookstore's role in helping the institution connect to all of its constituents: faculty, students, staff, parents, alumni and the community as a whole."

—Paul Mares, CSP, NACS Professional Development Field Consultant, Poway, CA

"*Connections* presents an attitude for doing business that is crucial for any store, regardless of size or ownership. For privately-owned stores, maintaining strong relationships with our customers, and a cooperative atmosphere with the campuses we serve is especially important."

—Harris D. Smithson, President/ General Manager, L & M Bookstore, San Antonio, TX

NACS/CSREF Publications & Resources

For a complete listing of NACS/CSREF industry resources including booklets, training videos, background information kits, and market surveys available to help you in making connections, order from the NACS Publications & Video Resources Catalog. Or, use this convenient order form to request publications specifically mentioned in *Connections: NACS & You.*

College Store Planning: A Mission and Vision Kit   Item #2239
  Price $59.95

College Store Service Quality Surveys Background Information Kit
Item #2193
  Member Price: $35
  Nonmember Price: $75

College Store Service Quality Research Kit   Item #2200
When ordering, be sure to specify your software choice of either IBM-PC/Compatible (5 1/4") Item #2202, *IBM-PC/Compatible (3 1/2")* Item #2203, *or Apple Macintosh* Item #2201.
  Price: $59.95

Colleges, Universities, and Institutional Stores: Partners in Higher Education Background Information Kit   Item # 2131
  Member Price: $35
  Nonmember Price: $75

Connections: NACS & You
Item #2322
  Price: $35

Considerations In College Store Renovation and Design
Item #1993
  Member Price: $35
  Nonmember Price: $75

Custom Publishing Background Kit
Item #2205
  Member Price: $35
  Nonmember Price: $75

Links: Faculty, College Stores, Publishers, and Students   Item #41
  Member: Qty 1-49 @ $2.00 ea.
  Nonmember: Qty 1-49 @ $5.00 ea.

1994 NACS Annual Financial Survey
Item #2079
  Member Price: $50
  Nonmember Price: $175

Service Quality Means Survival for Your Store - monograph
Item #2230
  Price: Packet of 5 @ $20;
      10 @ $30; 15 @ $37.50;
      20+ @ $2.00 per monograph

Service Quality Means Survival for Your Store - video
Item #2220
  Price: $20

The 1990's College Store Leadership Challenge: Achieving Excellence Through People
Item # 2215
  Price: Qty 1-5 @ $4.00 each;
      Qty 6 or more @ $2.50 each

Turning Points: Six Critical Challenges for College Stores
Item #2218
  Price: $35

You Can Make a Difference - video
Item #2219
  Member Price: $59.95
  Nonmember Price: $99.95

HOW TO ORDER

1. List the item number, description, quantity, and price of the items you'd like to order. The order form can be photocopied for future orders.

2. Choose your payment option. NACS members may choose to be billed. If you choose the credit card option, please provide your signature, along with your account number and expiration date.

3. Don't forget to indicate how you'd like to have the merchandise shipped. If you don't let us know, we'll automatically ship RPS ground.

4. Ready to order? Great! Take your pick of three convenient methods.

BY PHO
800/622-7
216/775-7
Ext. 3

BY FAX
216/775-4

BY MAI
NACS M
500 E. Lo
Oberlin, C
44074-12

ORDER FORM

❏ Bill me (NACS members only)   ❏ Check enclosed (made payable to NACS)
❏ Charge my: ❏ Visa ❏ MasterCard ❏ American Express

Card # _____ Exp. Date _____

Name as it appears on card _____

Signature _____

P.O. # _____ NACS # _____

Name _____

Store/Company Name _____

Address _____

City/State/Zip _____

Phone _____ Shipping method: _____

Item #	Title	Qty.	Price	Total

Shipping charges will be add